Last Words

Also by William S. Burroughs:

Last Words
The Final Journals of William S. Burroughs

Edited and with an Introduction by
James Grauerholz

Grove Press
New York

Published simultaneously in Canada
Printed in the United States of America

FIRST EDITION

Library of Congress Cataloging-in-Publication Data
Burroughs, William S., 1914–97
    Last words : the final journals of William S. Burroughs, November
1996–July 1997 / edited and with an introduction by James
Grauerholz.
        p.   cm.
    ISBN 0-8021-1657-4
    1. Burroughs, William S., 1914–97 Diaries. 2. Novelists,
American—20th century Diaries.   I. Grauerholz, James.   II. Title.
PS3552.U75Z468   2000
818'.5403—dc21
[B]   99-44259
                                                                   CIP

DESIGN BY LAURA HAMMOND HOUGH

Grove Press
841 Broadway
New York, NY 10003

00 01 02 03   10 9 8 7 6 5 4 3 2 1

Acknowledgments

William Burroughs's closest friends often saw him scribbling in the bound journal books that accumulated until there were eight of them, but he was a bit secretive about their contents. He did turn over one book to Jim McCrary to be typed up, and he made some editing marks on the transcription; this shows that he knew the journals would someday be published. (Selections from that typed journal were published in *The New Yorker* just after William's death, as "Last Words.") In late August 1997 Jim offered to transcribe the handwritten journals, and I was content for him to do that because I was not yet ready to face their contents, in William's familiar scrawl—"dead fingers talk."

I procrastinated reviewing Jim's transcription until the spring of 1999, when I finally felt up to the sad task of reading my best friend's last testament. Rather than silently correct mistakes of spelling or sense, I used brackets to insert short clarifications, or to indicate words and passages that remained illegible after my best efforts to decipher them. In the subsequent editing process (with Ira Silverberg's help), I cut about 5 percent of the material, primarily for reasons of privacy or because of excessive repetition. Following William's text in this volume is a set of editor's notes, arranged chronologically, providing additional background and explanation of his many references that would otherwise be obscure.

I must gratefully acknowledge the patience of my editors at Grove Press during this process, and especially Ira Silverberg, who signed this book for Grove and who encouraged and gently prodded me over the two years that it has taken me to complete it.

Jim McCrary's original transcription was a tremendous help, and a preliminary text-comparison review by Aaron Howard was also helpful. Barry Miles offered valuable corrections to my editor's notes. I was traveling for a long time while working on this book, and for their hospitality on the road I am especially grateful to: Diane de Rooy in Seattle; Gus Van Sant in Portland; Kathelin Gray in Berkeley; Stanley and Elyse Grinstein in Malibu; Steven Lowe in Truth or Consequences, N.M.; Mark Henning in Chicago; and Robert Lococo in St. Louis. For their ongoing assistance in the management of the many literary and artistic materials that William left behind, I am pleased to thank Andrew Wylie and Jeffrey Posternak at The Wylie Agency.

Introduction:
His Education

At the end of his life William Burroughs was living in Lawrence, Kansas, in a modest two-bedroom cottage built in 1929 from a Sears & Roebuck house kit on Learnard Avenue, a quiet residential street in an old part of town. His front porch was obscured from the roadway by a profusion of honeysuckle, trumpet vine and redbud, white cedar and hackberry trees, and to the south a wide creek ran through branches and poison ivy to a 1930s-era concrete culvert bridge. The house was painted brick red with white trim, its roof a simple full gable front to back. The square pillars supporting his porch had tilted slightly outward over the years, giving the front aspect a warped perspective. A white trellis on the south side of the porch was covered with red rose blooms every summer.

On the porch by Burroughs's front door there was almost always a cat sprawled out, sometimes two or three. A slab of soft marble lying by the door (an engraving sample from a funerary monument company) read BUR-ROSE. Behind the storm door the entry door was black, with a sticker on it to alert emergency authorities that there were cats inside to be saved. Through six beveled crystal panes in the upper door a distorted view of the interior showed a front room joining a dining area, with the tiny, brightly lit kitchen behind. A walnut buffet just inside the door was covered with an array of curios and talismans (a scorpion in Lucite, a curving kris, a jointed wooden snake); next to that, a cane stand was filled with a dozen walking sticks, clubs and canes with strange, carved handles. And an always-burning lamp on the small dining table might illuminate William Burroughs, hunched over in his four-wheeled "post-operative" chair, squinting at a paperback or scribbling in a bound journal book.

This is the view that greeted many an expectant visitor, for in the sixteen years after Burroughs moved to Lawrence at age sixty-seven he received countless pilgrims to his Midwestern *Alamout*—travelers from all over, mostly young people, seeking a brief personal contact with the author of *Naked Lunch*. His little house was the center of a continual round of social activity, with frequent visits by his many Lawrence friends and lively dinner company assured every evening. The daily shopping, cooking, and cleanup were handled by a rotating cast of regular companions, who often helped Burroughs host dinners for the many old friends who journeyed to Lawrence to spend time with him.

The most frequent visitors over the years were the poets John Giorno and Allen Ginsberg. After the "River City Reunion" in Lawrence in 1987—a weeklong gathering of poets and performers in William's honor—Allen began to make annual visits, on his way to or from Naropa Institute's summer writing program in Boulder, Colorado. When he was in Kansas Ginsberg stayed with Burroughs, the ex-lovers of years past now become two little old men sitting at the breakfast table in their bathrobes, arguing good-naturedly about nutrition and politics. Both were members of the American Academy of Arts and Letters, as well as the French Ordre des Arts et des Lettres, among other honors, but in William's modest "home on the range," far from the glare of celebrity, they renewed and continued a relationship that had begun during World War II.

In July 1996, at the age of eighty-two, Burroughs was honored with "Ports of Entry," a visual overview of his career at the Los Angeles County Museum of Art, curated by Robert Sobieszek. Ginsberg was with him for the opening and other festivities, and when the retrospective moved to the Spencer Museum of Art at the University of Kansas in early November of that year, he came to Kansas to take part in a symposium at the Kansas Union. Ginsberg spoke lovingly of his old friend to a full house, and William climbed to the stage for an embrace that was roundly cheered. Two days later Allen left for New York. Although Allen had been ill with diabetes and heart trouble for some time, there was no obvious reason to expect that this would be their last farewell.

William's health was still fairly good; it had been five years since his triple bypass operation, and while his energy reserves were clearly ebbing, his spirits were good. He was restless to be writing and keeping busy, and he said he was trying to reach a new synthesis of writing and painting, but without feeling that he had succeeded. Between diminished stamina and the arthritis in his hands, William had become unable to type more than a few lines. He often jotted down his thoughts—and, as always, his dreams—on index cards, but it was impossible to keep track of these or put them in any order. After our colleague Jim McCrary and I tried in vain to find a new typewriter that William could use, the idea arose to furnish him with bound blank books, in place of the index-card system.

It was in mid-November 1996 that Burroughs began to write the journals that are presented in this book. The first entry records the death of his cat, Calico Jane. In 260 days from November 14, 1996, to August 1, 1997, he made 168 entries. These writings include successive drafts of several short routines; remarks on books he was reading or had read long ago, and scenes suggested by them; lists of favorite lines from a lifetime of reading and listening; fits of impotent rage at man's stupidity; day-to-day commentary; the heartbreak of the deaths of his beloved cats; and the contemplation of his own mortality. As late as these last nine months of his life, Burroughs was still compelled to do imaginary battle with his primordial foes: "Drug Warriors," school-stupid FBI men, cat-haters, humans destroying the earth's species in their arrogance: "When whales and seals and elephants weep, I cannot suppress the deadly Sin of Anger."

The significance of William's empathy with animals cannot be overstated. "My relationship with cats has saved me from a deadly and pervasive ignorance," he wrote in notes for *The Cat Inside,* begun in 1982 at "the Stone House" south of Lawrence. As related in that short book, he was befriended soon after his arrival in Lawrence by three or four stray cats. When he moved into town to Learnard Avenue he brought along his favorite: Ruski, a Russian Blue. William had not always been a cat-lover, far from it; although he shuddered to remember it, he had several times been cruel to cats in Texas and Mexico. But now he thought often of the many people in his life who had died, and the cats seemed to represent them for him.

At his house on Learnard Avenue with its deep backyard garden, William took in a longhaired orange female stray whom he named Ginger. She mated with Ruski and produced "the orange litter," which included Calico Jane. The all-black Fletch was a foundling in downtown Lawrence in 1984, and he quickly became William's new favorite. Jane bore a litter to Fletch, and William gave the kittens to me and other friends. A male that William called Thomas appeared and disappeared in 1985–86, but another refugee, Mutie, a bulbous orange female tabby, stayed on after mating with Thomas. Her litter was distributed among friends, except for Senshu, the gray tabby female, who spent her life with William and her mother Mutie. After William brought Fletch into the house, the aging Ruski became undomesticable and he was farmed out to friends at a cabin on Lone Star Lake. It was around this time that William realized the folly of his prejudice against neutering his cats, and thereafter the only new addition to the cat family was Spooner, a longhaired gray-and-white male who was very affectionate.

Keeping all these cats in his small home, with cat-doors arranged to allow them to come in and go out at will, created a situation marked by frequent cat-feeding interruptions, continual feline vomiting and squabbling, and a house steeped with the rank smell of cat piss. (William had decided that old Calico was too feeble to make it outside for her evacuations and set up a litter box for her in his living room.) These animals, in their innocent wisdom, became William's all-day companions, sometimes his trial by distraction, and the objects of his heart's affection. He fed them compulsively, so that the two who were predisposed to overeating—Fletch and Mutie—eventually became quite rotund. And he showered them with jovial verbal abuse: "Come here you little whore, you little bitch . . ." But no sooner would he see one of his cats appear than he'd jump up to feed it and pet it. William doted on his cats.

What was William Burroughs's view of old age? For many years his primary, recurring literary protagonist—"Kim/Audrey"—was a version of himself in puberty and adolescence, but by the time he turned seventy his new work offered a series of middle-aged and elderly protagonists. Beginning in his late fifties with *Ah Pook Is Here* (1972) and continuing through the trilogy that began with *Cities of the Red Night* (1981), the idea of Death as a mythic antagonist had emerged as a central theme. In his later years Burroughs became preoccupied with the quasi-mystic Shootist *gestalt* of the Old West, and the elaborate "immortality blueprints" of the ancient Egyptians, with their mummies and their ontology of seven souls—a schema that Burroughs absorbed and adapted to his own literary purposes after reading Norman Mailer's *Ancient Evenings*. In a passage from *The Place of Dead Roads* (1984)—a work-in-progress that was a staple of Burroughs's many stage performances in the early 1980s—he makes an explicit statement of his ideas about immortality:

> Kim has never doubted the possibility of an afterlife or the existence of gods. In fact he intends to become a god, to shoot his way to immortality, to invent his way, to write his way. [. . .] Kim considers that immortality is the only goal worth striving for.

In *Dead Roads,* vacillating between his two personas—the persisting, unbearably radiant and amoral adolescent, Kim, and a new middle-aged figure, Joe the Dead, whose existence through many lifetimes has brought him to a desiccated, morbid condition —Burroughs clings to the viewpoint of Kim, despite the ever-widening gap between Kim's age and his own:

> Don Juan lists three obstacles or stages: Fear . . . Power . . . and Old Age.
> Kim thought of old men with a shudder: drooling tobacco juice, spending furtive hours in the toilet crooning over their shit. . . . The only old men that were bearable were *evil* old men like the Old Man of the Mountain [Hassan i Sabbah] . . . [. . .]
> So Kim splits himself into many parts . . . He hopes to achieve a breakthrough before he has to face the terrible obstacle of old age. . . . [. . .]
> It is said that Waghdas [the city of enlightenment] is reached by many routes, all of them fraught with hideous perils. Worst of all, Kim thinks, is the risk of being trapped by old age in a soiled idiot body like Somerset Maugham's. [. . .]
> Maugham would cower in a corner whimpering that he was a horrible and evil man.

He was, Kim reflected with the severity of youth, not evil
enough to hold himself together . . .

Kim is killed in a shoot-out at the Boulder Cemetery on the last
page of *Dead Roads*—but not by the other duelist, who is also shot
dead, both slain by a mysterious sniper. Near the beginning of *The
Western Lands* (1987), the last book of the Red Night trilogy, the
author reveals who has shot them both: Joe the Dead, a shadowy
character in *Dead Roads* whose life was saved by Kim, but only
after he was horribly burned and maimed, and who worked for Kim
and his gang. Here is Burroughs's explanation of Joe's motives and
his existential condition:

> Joe understood Kim so well that he could afford to dispense
> with him as a part of himself not useful or relevant at the present
> time. He understood Kim's attempt to transcend his physical
> structure, to which he could never become reconciled, by an
> icy, inhuman perfection of attitude, painfully maintained and
> refined to an unbearable pitch. Joe turned to a negation of at-
> titude, a purity of function that could be maintained only by
> the pressure of deadly purpose. [. . .]
>
> This continual pain is a sanction imposed by Nature, whose
> laws he flouts by remaining alive. Joe's only lifeline is the love
> of certain animals. [. . .]
>
> Cats see him as a friend. They rub against him purring, and
> he can tame weasels, skunks and raccoons. He knows the lost
> art of turning an animal into a familiar. The touch must be very
> brave and very gentle.

In this passage we see an accurate snapshot of the elderly
Burroughs himself, living alone with his cats and looking back
on his life. The adolescent "Kim" has finally succumbed to the

very personas into which he split himself, the representatives of the aging author.

> Don Juan says that every man carries his own death with him at all times. The impeccable warrior contacts and confronts his death at all times, and is immortal. [. . .]
>
> As Joe moves about the house making tea, smoking cigarettes, reading trash, he finds that he is, from time to time, holding his breath. At such times a sound exhales from his lips, a sound of almost unbearable pain. [. . .] What is wrong? To begin with, the lack of any position from which anything can be seen as right. He cannot conceive of a way out, since he has no place to leave from. His self is crumbling away to shreds and tatters, bits of old songs, stray quotations, fleeting spurts of purpose and direction sputtering out to nothing and nowhere, like the body at death deserted by one soul after the other.

On the first page of *My Education: A Book of Dreams* (1995), Burroughs recounts a dream remembered from thirty-five years before, shortly after the publication of *Naked Lunch* with the Olympia Press in Paris in 1959:

> Airport. Like a high school play, attempting to convey a spectral atmosphere. One desk onstage, a gray woman behind the desk with the cold waxen face of an intergalactic bureaucrat. She is dressed in a gray-blue uniform. Airport sounds from a distance, blurred, incomprehensible, then suddenly loud and clear. "Flight sixty-nine has been—" Static . . . fades into the distance . . . "Flight . . ."
>
> Standing to one side of the desk are three men, grinning with joy at their prospective destinations. When I present myself at the desk, the woman says: "You haven't had your education yet."

The curriculum of this education was soon revealed: he would live on, long enough to see most of his closest human friends, and all but two of his beloved animal companions, cross over to the Land of the Dead.

The suicide of Michael Emerton at age twenty-six in November 1992 was the first devastating loss in these final years. Michael had been my partner for almost eight years; he and William had become very close. Just over a year later, as William and I were finally recovering from this shock, William's first cat, the Russian Blue who had been the catalyst for the late-life opening of William's tender emotions, died in early 1994. Ruski's burial established the location of William's "cat cemetery," just south of a small pond that lies outside the window of his bedroom. Soon after Ruski's death, a new stray appeared, and William named him Spooner. At the height of his menagerie in the mid-1990s, William had six cats: Ginger, Fletch, Calico, Mutie, Senshu, and Spooner. But inevitably his cats began to die: Spooner succumbed to feline leukemia in early 1996, and a year later Senshu was swept away by a flash flood in the little creek.

Calico Jane's death in mid-November was just two weeks before the "Ports of Entry" show closed with The Nova Convention Revisited, a gala tribute to Burroughs at the University's Lied Center for the Performing Arts. The performers were old friends of his, veterans of the Nova Convention of 1978 in New York; the house was packed, and William was touched by the community's outpouring of affection and admiration. Two months later, in early February 1997, his eighty-third birthday was observed by a quiet gathering of friends in his home.

On a typical day in the last year of William Burroughs's life he would awaken in the early morning and take his methadone (he became re-addicted to narcotics in New York in 1980, and was on a maintenance program the rest of his life) and then return to bed. If the day were Thursday, I would arrive at 8:00 A.M. to drive him to his clinic in Kansas City, or—after he had finally earned a biweekly pickup schedule—take him out to breakfast, so that his house could be cleaned. At about 9:30 A.M. on all other mornings William would arise and—in his slippers, pajamas, and dressing gown—make his breakfast, sometimes a salted soft-boiled egg with toast, or perhaps fresh-squeezed lemonade, and two cups of very sweet tea. Feeding his many cats at the beginning of each day took up considerable time, only after which would he shave and dress himself, by about noon.

William might have visitors at midday, or he might make an outing to his friend Fred Aldrich's farm for some target shooting with other gun enthusiasts. Otherwise, he passed the afternoon looking through his gun magazines or reading an endless stream of books, sometimes works of serious fiction but more often in the category of pulp fiction, with an emphasis on medical thrillers, stories about police and gangsters, and—his favorite—science-fiction scenarios of plague ravaging the world. William's later novels demonstrate his fascination with "last words" and the nature of death, and he accumulated quite a library of books on the subject; for example: *They Went That-a-way; Famous Last Words; Weird Ways to Die; Until You Are Dead; The Egyptian Book of the Dead; How Did They Die, Volumes One and Two; Death and Consciousness; Sudden and Awful: American Epitaphs and the Finger of God; Death in Ancient Egypt; How We Die; The Abolition of Death; Life Without Death; What Survives?* William liked to go outside in the afternoon and walk in his garden, sometimes practicing throwing a knife into a board propped up against the little garage. But in his last year, he could usually be found lying down for an afternoon nap of an hour or two. One or more of his friends would arrive at 5:00 or 6:00 P.M. to join him for cocktails and make dinner. William's daily cocktails—which had started religiously at 6:00 P.M. when I first met him in 1974—now commenced at 3:30 sharp. After the first vodka-and-Coke and a few puffs on a joint, he often wrote in his new journal books until he was joined by his dinner companions.

William's physical condition was markedly improved after his recovery from the 1991 coronary bypass, but he suffered from a painful hiatal hernia, intermittent arthritis, and cataracts in both eyes. He was barrel-chested but very thin and stooped, yet amazingly energetic and agile for his age. He surprised many a visitor by suddenly—for effect—brandishing a sword concealed in a cane, or a blackjack, or a new knife in his collection. He was always jumping up and rushing into other rooms, sometimes talking as he went, as if his guests were meant to follow. During the cocktails-and-dinner hour he had a marked tendency to monologue, but in his last year he became more patient and attentive to his dinner companions.

In this last year William conserved his strength by "making an early evening of it," sometimes starting to take off his shirt at 8:30 or 9:00 P.M. to signal his guests that they should move their fellowship elsewhere. During the night he was, by his own account, up out of bed many times to urinate or deal with cat exigencies. He often said he was a light sleeper, and until the middle of the night he was, but he usually slept soundly for several hours in the early morning hours, curled up on his side in a fetal position, his hands tucked between his thighs—and his pistol under the covers, not far from his hand, in case of trouble.

The spring of 1997 turned ominous with the unexpected death in late March of our friend, Lawrence architect John Lee, at fifty-one. In the preceding year William's old friends Herbert Huncke, Terry Southern, and Timothy Leary had died. Now Allen Ginsberg was in the hospital in New York, and William was in touch with him by telephone. Despite encouraging signs, Allen's doctors discovered widespread liver cancer and predicted he had only a few months to live. The shock of this news was followed closely by Allen's sudden death just a week later, on April 5, 1997. William was stunned by Allen's disappearance; his own mortality had never seemed so close at hand. It was clearly the end of an era. Journalists plagued William for his response to his old friend's death, and he furnished them a statement that cannot have come close to expressing his inner feelings.

On May 24th, forty-nine days after Allen's death (the period prescribed in the *Tibetan Book of the Dead* as the length of a dead soul's wanderings in the *bardo*), our friend Wayne Propst hosted a "Bardo Burn" for Allen at his home, north of Lawrence. More than a hundred friends from the community took part in the symbolic immolation of numerous images of Allen, in a purpose-built "fire cage." William read aloud from the first part of Allen's "Howl" to the assembled group, and then joined them in eating and drinking —a proper Lawrence wake. But the equanimity with which William seemed to accept his old friend's passing was later revealed in these journals to have covered a profound inner sorrow and sense of loss.

That summer was lively and filled with visitors to Lawrence, notably our old friends Steven Lowe and Ira Silverberg. Ira and I spent two weeks selecting the passages from William's oeuvre that became *Word Virus: The William S. Burroughs Reader*, published by Grove Press in 1998. Ira's arrival was just two days after Fletch, William's companion for thirteen years since he first appeared as a lithe young kitten, died of heart failure and obesity on July 9, 1997. This loss seems to have hastened William's own end, which came just three weeks later.

* * *

My high charms work,
And these mine enemies are all knit up
In their distractions: they now are in my power . . .

These lines from Shakespeare's *The Tempest* might stand for Burroughs's entire literary project after *Naked Lunch* and the Cut-Up trilogy. His works from the mid-1960s onward frankly essay the rewriting of human (and his own) history, righting their manifold wrongs by un-writing them. After a long obsession with weapons and conflict, Burroughs became politicized during the 1960s and openly aspired to change cultural reality with his books. Two decades after he returned to the United States in 1974 and began the most public phase of his artistic career, he had the satisfaction of seeing his life's work reflected throughout the society and culture of the late twentieth century.

In his last year William often quoted these lines from Tennyson's "Ulysses": "How dull it is to pause, to make a rest / To rust unburnish'd, not to shine in use." His efforts now were inward, as he sifted through memories of his long life and cast about him for a worthy opponent against whom to go on doing battle. In his journals he rails against the bottomless stupidity of humankind—he was still fighting the good fight, still working for human liberation. But William's greatest struggle was against the "rotten weeds" of his own human failings, and the effort to prepare himself to face his final confrontation: the end that he knew was coming. These journals show his growing awareness that, rather than "rage against the dying of the light," he must surrender to the inevitable, a battle that could be won only by laying down his arms.

As the winter of 1996–97 turns into spring, William's fury gradually disappears from these pages. With insight into the reflexes of his unruly "Ugly Spirit," he writes: "Always the cloth: *'Toro! Toro!'* and one charges again and again." In these last months of his life he seems weary of his old hatreds, and eager to say, with Prospero, at last: "But this rough magic / I here abjure." He sees the emptiness of anger and conflict, the illusory nature of victory and vengeance, and in his last days he realizes: "Thinking is not enough. Nothing is. There is no final enough of wisdom, experience—any fucking thing. No Holy Grail, No Final Satori, no final solution. Just conflict. Only thing can resolve conflict is love, like I felt for Fletch and Ruski, Spooner and Calico. Pure love."

In the last years of his life William Burroughs was allowed—by effort, suffering, and grace—to finish his education.

—James Grauerholz,
SUMMER 1999

Last Words

the apo-morphine doctor — you
think it cured me? It doesn't at
all. So where'd
you got ten to
serve Denver,
Fred Bopler?
He doesn't move
in my circles.
He'd just seen
his hang foot?
Killey
Freud
in
the
chair
and his
own
hair
stood
up and
chuckled
with joy.

Just other day
I witness to
Texas lethal
injection. he
~~kidicated~~
resulted raising
his arms
"Was it good?"

Thursday This is November 14, 1996.

November 10, Calico was killed at 19th and Learnard. I heard about it the 12th from José. Tom had seen the cat by side of the road.

In the empty spaces where the cat was, that hurt *physically*. Cat is part of me. Mornings since, I break into uncontrollable sobbing and crying when I remember [where] she used to be—sit—move, etc. No question of histrionics. It just happens.

So dream remembered:

Oh, it was also a cat. I wasn't sure it could find its way.

November 15, 1996. Friday

Still hits whenever I see a place where she used to occupy.

The heart doc says I am leaking.

Well, *"Qui vivre verra."*

November 16, 1996

Coming up narrow tenement stairs. Met two people coming down at landing, said: "Hello."

At top of stairs was a cubicle room with old sewing machine and other odds and ends, and there was an affectionate cat, whose head seemed removable. This room was open at top, three floors up.

Other people on roof said something about "Absolutely," referring to the cats.

Nov 17 or 18, 1996. Monday

Project: overheard, casual walking down 2nd Ave NYC. Two black guys pass, talking. One, in a white sweatshirt, says: "*Counselors* and all that shit."

Obviously talking about the Methadone program. How some black voices can cut right to the bone through all the bullshit.

"Very dangerous."

William Bennett, late—I hope, certainly former—Drug Czar under Reagan and Bush. He continues: "We must target the 'casual user.'"

"Which is it this time, Holmes? Cocaine or morphine?"

"Both, Watson, a speedball."

Casual users who hold jobs and manage their lives successfully (like me) send a message that people can use illegal drugs and still function adequately.

"Very dangerous."

Dangerous to whom exactly, Mr. Bennett? Very dangerous to liars like Bennett and Anslinger and the whole ill-intentioned and downright evil cluster of fiends born from the Harrison Narcotics Act. A vast hierarchy of evil, from street narcs working their snitches to kids turning in their parents.

"The War Against Drugs has united us as a nation."

Bush or Reagan—take your pick.

A nation of what? Stool pigeons? Informers?

I like the Russian word for "informer": *stukach*. A word to be spit.

Our pioneer ancestors would puke in their graves.

"Very dangerous."

What is this asshole Bennett, who smokes two packs of cancer a day, really saying? To be a good American you have to be a goddamn liar? Of course people live to ripe and productive old age on junk. Look at Herbert Huncke, 81; De Quincy, 74; George Crabbe, English poet, 78; and yours truly, [82] and still kicking.

Turn-of-the-century physician who treated a number of morphine addicts said: "The general health of the morphine addict is excellent."

"Very dangerous."

Nixon said that Tim Leary, old friend of mine, was "the most dangerous man in America." Dangerous to whom, exactly? To a blueprint for an international police state under cover of a total drug war.

A bit late to hit the barricades and paving stones. Maybe two hundred years ago—already arresting "drug dealers" in other countries. (Suppose some greasy spic narcs should have dragged Reagan out of the White House for undisclosed offenses?)

And an old queen is hauled before a Dutch court for "minor incidents" in the Philippines.

"Very dangerous."

To queens who batten on these Moors in Morocco and elsewhere.

"This international parasitism is a very bad thing."

Dr. John Yerbury Dent was the least paranoid of men, and he had the full warmth and goodwill, the best the English can offer.

He said: "I think what the American narcotics people are doing is bad."

He didn't want to use the word: Evil. But I do. Evil for anything Homo Sap may have created or may hope to create. I mean Evil, Evil, Evil—implemented by corrupt, evil, sadistic individuals.

Always accuse others of what you (the liar) are doing. Not to go into the media of it, that rancid old *cenote*, bubbling up belches of coal gas from rotten lungs and guts. Nothing good is bubbling up here.

November 19, 1996. Tuesday

Lake or river with patches of algae on top. I swim across to a wooden dock avoiding the algae.

Another lake with clear water. I can see down to clusters of goldfish 20 feet [below], and between.

Walking (wrong number, Harris Construction) back to the Bunker. Tried a shortcut through a Turkish Bath that opens on a closet, that opens on the hall at 222 Bowery. Decide not to take the Turkish shortcut.

"I got twenty-three dope fiends in here now."

(Harried attendant at the Lexington Narc hospital.)

In a dream last night (Nov. 18, Monday) I was a cop. I said:

"I got a gun and I got a baton. I need handcuffs and a two-way radio."

Standing at counter waiting for my radio and handcuffs, pepper gas and other good things.

"Very dangerous" for Bennett and Co., that any man could feel a basic, deep, real emotion like grief, heartbreak, the joy that comes from danger and death.

"Is it not fine to dance and sing

While the bells of death do ring?"

"Very dangerous"

"Bring out your dead."

The heart of the matter.

Desertion: Waiting day after day, tomorrow and tomorrow, hope always dimmer, further away.

"I was waiting there."

Let he who created a world of sin and stones cast the first stone.

Nothing under the mask but Death.

Bennett & Co deplore relative ethics. They want absolute. All right, let's get absolute:

What they are doing is *WRONG, EVIL,* by any human standards.

Tomorrow, November 20, 1996

It was a Wednesday and Victor Bockris will give me a medal for longevity.

You just live long enough and you will become the grand old man of letters a bit tired with his very tired old jokes. Some bordering on the *risqué*.

(The grand old man of letters will accrete around you with cashmere shawls.)

The man in a cheap hotel makes it with lady in next room. Next day as they meet on a landing, she says: "*Bonjour, Monsieur,*" wiggling her little finger suggestively. He responds by taking off his hat and placing the top side over his crotch: "*Bonjour, Madame!*"

Well, I guess my Pullman car joke is a bit heavy for a mixed audience. Or the one about animals checking their equipment and some character has the elephant's [trunk]. Don't clearly see the point in that one.

Any case, back at a party in the 30s and there was someone there who could—*and unfortunately did*—imitate Roosevelt:

"My friends, I hate war. Eleanor hates war. And I hate Eleanor."

Heh, heh. It was a long time ago, and it wasn't funny even then.

And what has become of the *New Yorker* cartoons? They are not funny or even comprehensible any more. Where are the classic cartoons of Charles Addams and Peter Arno?

Yes, where are the snows of yesteryear. And the speedballs I useta know?

Well, I guess it's time for my Ovaltine and a long good night.

"Well just who are you?"

"Come in please."

The name is Sam Beckett, of course.

So back to basics—anything etc. The simple concept of a "decent person." You can see it is the best of the English. It is self-evident.

"You I cannot help but see. . . ."

Old props falling from East St. Louis, to Shanghai to Panama, NYC, London, through London—come through, London:

"Loud and clear."

"How can I know?"

One outpost of joy from within is a deadly threat to the invading, invaders, who are?

Are, our, the voices, creaks—they must eliminate.

This "just want to live over here and do our thing" is absolutely intolerable to the invaders.

I can see their radar screen picking up José and me coming back from the Methadone Clinic. Funny thing, that cop never looked at me. Never asked José what in hell Burroughs Communications was? And I would have to stand forth and say:

"*I am* William Burroughs. I communicate."

How often on undercover [assignment] on this planet is one tempted to use "Deadly Force."

Get a hold on yourself, young man, and lie straight. What they call truth here is lie there—their lie.

"Our sacred truth. We'll die for it if given the chance."

Sorry, they aren't fitted even for the hawg-pen of Creation.

Wednesday November 20, 1996.

Dream of sex that cannot be realized for some reason. No connection with waking consciousness.

"That old feeling." Complete with self-pity.

"That old feeling is still in my leaking heart."

Hmm. Who was it. Composite, I guess.

Every time I put out three cat pans instead of four, the death of Calico hits again—or I see the place [where] she used to eat, beside the sink. All the empty places. *The memory of what has been and never more will be.* Killed by a car, she left with me all the places she used to be and never more would be.

If I thought the driver did it deliberately—if then I could find him—I have a catalogue here advertising a vial of Road Kill. A touch in his ear, on the porch, sent in envelopes under his door.

Well, can it. This is going nowhere, like the man whose child suffocated in an icebox HE himself had left out, chopping the box to pieces with an axe.

You don't get off that easy, pal. *Who* left the icebox out there?

Film—

A series of short takes—headlines—"Flight 800 lost over Atlantic."

Switch to airport: "Flight 800 now boarding at Gate 23."

Precognitive fear—now we come to the mushroom cloud that darkened the earth—Hiroshima.

Paul Bowles's dream: "Off the track! Off the track!"

Psychics, experts, scientists say the Earth will go out of orbit in the year 2000. Idiocy, War on Drugs—fear hanging over the planet. "The Man." "Yellow Peril"—etc.

Short, short cuts.

Plane—Pop singer takes shot in head. Shots in other times and places. (We see blood blossom in a million syringes, and hit home.)

Cuts to Doctor Kent—Painless Cure.

"Very dangerous."

The sickness of the world is junk—fear of, attempts to control and to spread, for excuse to control—

It's all so obvious—intelligent opposition from the Drug Policy Letter.

On plane—sleeping passengers—dream flashes.

"My creeping opponents say that I am trading on my reputation as a writer to gain notice as a painter. Of course I am. In this life, one is well advised to play the cards one has for all they are worth.

"If one is lucky enough to be born with a beautiful face and the corresponding physical attributes, instead of moaning 'Oh people only want me for my face,' play your face card. Youth plays the cards of youth and vitality—in youth, play your youth cards. In old age, claim the privileges of age, and get your snout in the public trough before it dries up.

"I want to thank all those who have made this show possible and contributed their expertise as performers, as curators and organizers. And in particular Robert Sobieszek, for a magnificent job [of] selecting and presenting the material at the L.A. County Museum of Art, the same show that is here now.

"And I thank sincerely those who have come here to perform this evening, and all of you who are here tonight."

November 29, 1996. Friday

"So laughable," she says.

It's the banishing ritual—ho ho ho, hum hum hum.

"Whatever comes . . . !"

Herr Professor Federn. Sure, it worked sometimes, back in the age of hysteria, dissociation, multiple personalities. Don't work now—like penicillin—

See "mental illness" as a vast organism dedicated to fuck up the Sapiens Project. How can an illness be "mental"? What [does] it *feed* on?

So for "mental" in the books, substitute "don't know" or "soul sickness."

So? I wonder.

Back at Chestnut Lodge. If I had stayed? Where would I be now?

Qui vivre verra.

It was not to be.

I like a weapon close to me
Because I am so cowardly
I have seen Fear
and Fear has made me free
Who lives will see
To look Death in the eye
With no Kamikaze lie
Wrap no flag around me
Who lives will see.
Man can be alone with Death
Will receive a second breath.

Café Lipp—hiking thru tall grass. I had forgotten my gun and [holster]. I was with someone indistinct—rummaging thru drawers, found only the .25. A deep wood drawer, completely empty.

"A Nothing Man" at the 1962 Writers Conference in Edinburgh. Put me on the literary map, thanks in part to Mary McCarthy, my spiritual sister—more than that—

What a job [she did] on the worst of the male sex: "The Young Man"—

A hospital for minor surgery. Hears screams in the night.

"The cancer patient at last!"

And he sang out *lustily:*

"Cast a cold eye on life, a cold eye on death—Horseman, pass by!"

No wonder for no apparent medical reason the surgeon could ascertain the young man's heart just stopped in mid-surgery.

I think for no reason to continue his lusty singing and to debase the human image by a hundred cuts. So horrible beyond realization —a shattered, falsified picture of a non-being. What force could so deform a man? Sucking screams off cancer patients, not even.

To nurse: "I heard screams last night, was that the cancer case?"

Nurse: "You'll never hear a sound from Mr. Miller, must have been in maternity."

"Oh."

The young man deflates like a pale green balloon.

"Oh, oh, oh."

"Well, it's time for your pre-operative medication."

Young man in a sudden panic.

"I, uh, well . . ."

Darkness creeps up from the front of his bed.

"I am the Captain of my soul," he mutters, as the stretcher slides down the hall, into an elevator—to the O.R.

In Tangier, my typewriter in hock to buy Eukodol, a chemical derivative of codeine, many times stronger. Dihydro-oxy-codeine— finally outlawed, owing to side effect of euphoria, hits like a speedball, Kid.

Guess I used all of it up in Tangier—but it's still out there in Quevedo, Ecuador, on a dusty back shelf, covered with mildew on a South Sea island—

"Shoot it in the main line, Kid. Hits like a speedball."

Maybe up in some Swede town under the Northern Lights— Christmas story.

"Any more of that?"

"Well yes—a consignment of twenty boxes—twenty in each box. Let you have it all for, well, say $100 U.S. dollars."

"Done."

Can we, the males, live without the other half? Female?

And O.H. must always talk. O.H. is talk, was the original invasion—was "word," of course, so cut word out in slow withdrawal.

It's going to hurt and hurt bad.

Saturday November 30, 1996.

I said: "L. Ron Hubbard needs a knife in his gizzard."

And I demonstrate with an assassin knife from Alamut how one strikes upward under the left rib cage to the heart. And I threw another knife into what looked like tinfoil.

Unpleasant feel of no meaning to me. Just floating by.

So to go on from here.

What is the "whatever comes?"

As Federn used to say in his study, [middle]-European apartment—rather like Schlumberger's in Paris—

Steak and bread and salad—red wine—talking to Allen Ginsberg about some English [person], says:

"A blues singer, a blues shouter. Everybody going to see my black bottom. He really gives out."

What, exactly?

Perhaps somewhere out there—Quevedo, Ecuador, *uno de puro*, Peru . . . on the back shelf a dusty box of ampules, Eukodol, 15 mg per ampule.

"Shoot it in the main linc, Kid, hits like a speedball."

Who. When where? Why?

Short stories?

Like the feeling there is some final resolution ahead—has to be?

"*Quién es?*" Last words of Billy the Kid. Garrett was very close, five feet, maybe. Couldn't miss.

The Secret Army?

I won't say "we lost," because some of what's left of us is still in there.

War stories—the room on top of the Lottery Bldg. in Tangier. John Hopkins came in and said from the balcony: "Looks like a naval battle."

(It had been a desperate engagement. Day after day the war.)

Heavy fog with holes in it, like artillery fire.

So what we got now?

Why not realize *their* pretext, and hit the Evil of the War Against Drugs. The sums involved in the money laundries are trillions of dollars, while people caught with an ounce of morphine are hanged.

Yes, the whole pestilent horde born from the Harrison Narc. Act is Evil with regard [to] anything Homo Sap can or will ever create—with regard [to] the space frontier. In a malignant intervention of Alien (to resident mammals) influence. And as usual Homo Sap laps it up as the right way to go.

"We'll build more prisons," Bush snarled.

"We already got one million inside."

(ref. *The Job*)

* * *

It was May 1, May Day, and all at once it just fell apart, the whole flimsy structure just collapsed like the proverbial house of cards.

No, it was not like a return to warlords. There just weren't any warlords left, or any other human roles. People fell apart like a rotten undervest, like rotten burlap, there wasn't anything left to hold them together. Only one thing did, that was war, and there was no more war. The only thing had kept the planet together (in a literal sense there are two halves magnetized together) was WAR. No more unemployment. Shit, nothing left to be employed for—groups of people strut about in improvised uniforms, waving rusty sabers.

"*Voici le sabre*
De mon pere."
Allons enfants de la patrie,
Les jours de gloire sont arriveé—
o'er the land of the free
and the home of the brave

Shall I hit the road against the Evil of the Drug War, the War Against Drugs—*Illegal* drugs. All right to smoke two packs of cigarettes a day as Bennett did or maybe does. *That legal.*

Well, the Evil—narc working his snitches for a buy, kids, after-school pep talk, turning in their parents for drugs. It's *EVIL.*

Not like "both sides of the question."

It's Evil, and the real $$$$$$$$ in Malaysia and Singapore and West Indies, Bahamas.

Target Lake Charles. Here Mel picked up a tracer. Port Arthur? Of course. Can feel it now. *Rauschmit!*—out with it!

So Mel, come in please. Mel, come on. Mel—come dirty.

"This is a fact, they kill you."

Who they, Mel? They same as people who conflict with . . .

"For chrissakes, don't do that."

I wouldn't ever do that.

What try get out.

No get. End.

"His macho quick-draw act too laughable for words."

I hear her loud and clear and—"rather amusing, going to abolish words"—bitching, waking up bitching the way Spanish wives do.

Be able to sit in silence on sand muted street for hours?

Why not? Other folk want to yack, let them.

I never indicated the *only* way to do or go anywhere. Shotgun art one of various random procedures—Pollock drip canvases, Yves Klein set his canvases on fire and put out the fire at the right moment.

November 30, 1996

Oh, last night a Turkish Bath scene, vaguely sexual—ho hum.

I [was an] ultimate monster or drug dealer, and a child molester. Am [a] crack addict, but that only a sideline.

He loved cats and ferrets, and weasels and all sneaky killing animals. And he was into crystal balls and ectoplasm and all that unwholesome stuff.

I repeat: What the American Narcotics Dept. is doing, did do and will do, is *Evil*. They insist on the lie of absolute right and wrong. They want absolutes—all right. Evil from the point of view of any decent person. From the street narcs working their snitches to the kids turning in their parents.

I'm an old-fashioned person, and I don't like informers. No matter how federal judges may be lenient with violators who have "cooperated" (rolled over) with authorities ("rolled over" is current phrase), and bear down heavy on those who "refuse to cooperate."

Dec 1, 1996. Sunday

In a plane coming in for a landing in Paris. The plane landed in a narrow slot. Outside I could see Paris streets and then the plane angled upwards, looked ready to stall at any moment, and I felt *physical fear*.

"It's going to crash!"

But it didn't crash. Landed OK in Paris.

Paris is in many ways my favorite city. Never really got into Rome. London was always antithetical to me. Leaving NYC which is always New York. Small towns like Tangier.

December 2, 1996. Monday

Enemy have two notable weaknesses:

1. No sense of humor. They simply don't get it.

2. They totally lack understanding of magic, and being totally oriented toward control, what they don't understand is a menace, to be destroyed by any means—consequently they tip their hand. They don't seem to care anymore—but famous last words: "We've got it made."

Deadly by the logic of fiction.

Just can't let them villains off scot-free?

Why Scot? Why not Swats, or Cot, Pot, Rot, Sot, slut, spot, shot, trot free—

Any case, they tend to overplay a hand. Ninety-nine percent bilious weasels.

It's slappable—

and who is here now?—

best I can—got it back.

You never really have it till you lose it, Fritz. Till you lose it and then get it back. Few make it back from that track, Jack.

"As to what life may be worth when the honor is gone. . . ."

(French Naval officer in *Lord Jim*. One of the great characters of fiction.)

And look at the others by Conrad: Councillor Mikulin from *Under Western Eyes*, the Nigger "Wait" from *Nigger of the Narcissus*. All touched with [the] hand of creation.

Many others of course, maybe just a walk-on.

Brion Gysin hated Denton Welch. Didn't see that it is just the petulant queerness in which he is straitjacketed—"Little Punky"—that makes his works such a great escape act.

Yes, for all of us in the Shakespeare Squadron, writing is just that: not an escape from reality, but an attempt to *change* reality, so [the] writer can escape the limits of reality.

The unworthies in power feel danger, like cows uneasily pawing the ground with a great "Moo."

The song of the quick
that is heard by the ears of the dead
the widows of Langley are loud in their wail
and the idols are broken in the temples of Yale
for the might of the Board
unsmote by the sword
has melted like snow
in the glance of the bored

Ho hum—
to look death in the eye,
with no posturing lie,
just one on one . . .
who lives will see.
Is Death an organism?

Way down in Tierra del Fuego—a lot of Eukodol ampules.

This horror of drugs, orchestrated by Hearst and his "yellow peril," then Anslinger—Harrison Narcotics Act—criminals by Act of Congress. You can't compare alcohol, cigarettes to narcotics. Why not? Because alcohol and tobacco are legal, that's why. What nonsense is here.

What they really can't understand is *division, possession*—or perhaps they understand all too well, and do not want [it] examined.

Tell any feminist I shot Joan in a state of possession, and she will scream:

"Nonsense! No such thing. HE did it."

Opera of the Angler Fish that absorbs the male till nothing is left of him but his testicles, balls, nuts, sticking out of her body.

All of me
why not take
all of me
so we become
one big WE
how great to be
one great fat me
Excuse me:
include me out.

December 5, 1996. Thursday

Now imagine a woman dancing out rug rat?

Well, it was like he was dancing [it] out in terrible agony, something in his spine, and the smell of rotten crabs, sweet gagging stench of excrement—and death.

After the shot he collapsed on the bed and lay there inert, but something was stirring in his spine from neck to the tail—and now pieces tore loose in the eggs and then a red, glistening head emerges in reeking yellow slime—and then the whole centipede, crawling out quick.

I got out my Detective Special. Then, moving with hideous speed and purpose, it scuttled through [the] ballroom screen.

"Head it off. Must kill it."

Too late, I turn back to the empty chrysalis of the body that once had been Parker, and even as I watched, the very flesh and bones disintegrated into a lost ballpoint pen on the floor.

Oh here it is—on the bed.

So.

December 8, 1996. Sunday

Dream last night that I was in a cubicle room with mosquitoes. (According to the news, Nov. 26, 1996: dreams of insects on one can precede a deadly illness. Recall another recent dream of biting flies.)

I take train for Manhattan. Got off at 10th Street. Can I walk from here to where?

Dec 9, 1986—hum—I mean '96
Check back on this date ten years ago.

In Paul's dream we see a *potential* scenario, which should be in-dicated by a special mode or style—screaming in all languages known and unknown, suddenly cut off—dimmed down—old man with cat. Has 1890s look:

"Is it the end, Holmes?"

"'Fraid so, old chap. Tried to get a warning out. No one *could* believe it. I mean, they were *designed* not to believe it."

"What do you propose to do, Holmes?"

"Nothing whatever, Watson. The time for intervention is gone."

Back to September 17, 1996:

He steps to his modest balcony: to the sky, the powerful and rich of the earth on their knees beg his help.

"Aw, why dontcha ask your mother," he snarls into the big mic, for all to hear.

The mob writhes forward, hands clasped in the [begging posture].

"*Please—*"

"'These are unsightly tricks,' in the words of the Immortal Bard."

Fear! What is fear of. What is subject afraid of? The unknown?

Of course not. The half-known, the you-don't-want-to-know. And what is that?

A reed in water—hieroglyph for "?"

Endangered hats on female heads shift in winds of instant fashion. Wives trail by each other at cocktails, *vernissages*, faster, faster—

"Off the track! Off the track!" Great chunks of suburban houses tilt, slide, crumble.

Present time feeling of being deracinated, without roots— moving—(someone just called for Jim Patterson. Wrong Jim. McCrary? Sorry)—moving where?

Mutie cat holds out paw as if to restrain me. Now she is purring round my feet. Took food to Ginger on front porch.

A sudden rent in the sky, clouds pulled in—the hole is more "real" than the sky.

December 11, 1996

Let the little growth on my head rest. It is an inoperable, benign, nonentity. So let it stay like that. If the soft machine works, don't fix it. If it works, don't fix it.

The words under the words, bubbling up with a belch of coal gas:

"We are—They are—come on! Hit! Hit!"

He cowered there, nursing the welt inflicted.

December 12, 1996

Story of the rich junky.

I [was] described by a moron critic as the world's richest ex-junky. If $1,500 in [the] bank and no other assets made me the richest.

Had I been as rich as I would have been if my father had kept his Burroughs stock (ten million $$ right there), *Naked*

Lunch would never have been written, nor any comparable work.

Show me a great writer very rich on inherited money. In France some good writers, like Gide, were *well off,* but not stratospheric rich.

Big $$ is a tight club. The staff has to be sure [the] applicant won't do anything contradictory to big money. Anything creative is not indicated and will not be tolerated.

Like what would I do if I were president. I would never be president. You gotta qualify, see. Same way with Big $ Daddy. I mean big enough to have political influence. Chemical Co. purchasing Apomorphine variations, and endorphin, etc. Own a newspaper, *that* kinda money.

No way he can get *that* $$ without the big OK, and without that $$ he's just an "eccentric."

Lovable, of course.

December 13, 1996

Tomorrow James's birthday—

Last night some sexy nonsense, no get—dreams about Mikey Portman, dead these many years.

So: "I paid for that C, Mikey, and I aims to use it."

Had to put my foot down heavy with Mikey. It was freezing, windy London night—down to get this C from this old coke hag, bugs was crawling out of her—

Her said: "Coke bugs, sure"—transparent.

December 14, 1996. James Day.

The story of the Burroughs Family. Vague, disreputable ghosts—
begging letters from widows of remote uncles:

"He was always kind to me except when—drinking—"

To set the record straight: William Seward Burroughs, who
created the first practical adding machine. Died in Citronelle,
Alabama, of TB age 41. He left four heirs: Horace, Mortimer,
Jennie, Helen.

Administrator of the estate had the word: "buy the family out—
$100,000 each." Big money in those days, when a silver dollar
bought a first-class meal couldn't be bought now for any price,
or a good piecea ass.

At the insistence of my mother, Dad held back a small block
of Burroughs stock. With remainder bought the Burroughs
Glass Co.

Facts. Bits of detail filter back from Mother. Dad had killed a
little colored boy years ago. Goes into a dark room, and there is
brother Horace with claws—

Mother on Horace:

"When he came into a room it was like someone had walked
out"—

Killed himself by breaking out a window and cut his wrists with
the glass shards—? Don't sound like a junky to me.

Horace here:

"It wasn't, Bill. They killed me. They is just who you think."

"Why? What about Helen? Horace—come in?"

Did he? Many long years ago—

Yagé mucho da.

Sees a fox.

"Why not?"

No dreams last night I can remember back now.

You got dope,

you got hope.

Just let your hand take over and . . .

"Easy, in any drugstore. Walk in, flash a fiver and—the morphine is right ready, and of course, the syringe."

First vein shot was an accident.

"Who cut into you Horace?"

He wasn't special, but he was always there—and that's a basic secret: *just be there.* He didn't cut his wrists.

Very confused images—ignorant Armies clash by night—

"It is getting just too tiresome."

Horace has a sort of English lower-class feel to his spirit—nasty and cheap, but he ain't lying when he says he was murdered. . . .

"You'll cover for us. Listen I run. We know, respectable. Well, let's keep it that way. Guy was depressed—and so . . . fill in the blanks."

Yeah, I guess.

What coulda done it?

Well, what did it.

The room could never be rented again. Roomer left after one night, complaining of showers of glass in dreams getting always more real, sharp.

Even so it's still weird.

So what. Articulate it.

How many species became extinct? And why?

About half a million, they tell me—always something inexpressibly sad about the last of a line.

December 15, 1996. Sunday

To miss a cat is to miss *your* cat, part of *you*.

It hurts physically, like an amputation. There on top of the sofa, on the side of the sink where she always ate. It hurts.

As Wordsworth, that old child molester, said:

"She died and left to me
this heath this calm this quiet scene
The memory of what has been
and never more will be."

Many spiritual disciplines establish as a prerequisite of advancement the attainment of inner silence. Rub out the word. Castaneda in *The Teachings of Don Juan* stresses the need to suspend the inner dialog—rub out the word—and gives precise exercises designed to attain a wordless state.

Rub out the word—laughable if you will, Leslie—

Alan—hear me?
Yes, William.
Well—the dream—don't surrender. It's a trick!
I went down under a hail of dream bullets. They don't kill. I had made my point and position clear. That P.P. very stratospheric, way out.

Any group acquires group markings. Feminists: self-righteous— able to believe any lie they have invented, utterly humorless— without honor or common decency in their dealing with the "sex enemy." It's just a bore—

Now the macho—John Wayne square-jawed, bigoted, stupid—insensitive—

So as soon you got a pressure you have an archetype.

December 16, 1996

Scientists are mired in respectability. Does it not penetrate their
skulls that some phenomena might only occur *once*? Or at a certain pattern *in time*—only every third Tuesday, etcetera.

And they have an insatiable appetite for Data: "More data!"
they scream, "and nothing anecdotal." (This may be the only data
in some cases.)

"Not conclusive!"

Is anything ever?

December 16, 1996

Reading account from 1879 settlers. Hospitable:

"Tie your horse and come in."

I always carried a gallon of whiskey to smooth things out.
Wouldn't say no to a shot of whiskey? They wouldn't.

Of course the dog always announced my arrival. Principal function of country dog to give notice of approach.

"Pays the hand $15 per month. Pays me $5 per month for your
sleeping and breakfast here."

Them was the days.

Dream last night. John de—no sex—and water again last night.
I was holding onto the bowsprit—which dunked into the water
sometimes.

Always these dreams of water, dirty, clear, deep blue—waters deep blue.

December 17, 1996. Tuesday

Cold heavy depression now. Disintegrating—into grass with snow, making old gentlemen with white whiskers.

Gray clouds—black branches—water ebbing, leaves, then:

"Me stranded—"

I told "me" so—

"The razor inside sir, jerk the handle."

I just did, and it all leaked out like hydraulic fluid and I said: "Let it go"—

And I went and I laughed like the little boy on the ghost horse—laughing a laugh that was not of this world.

(Entire story one of the best in this genre, like Radiant Boys.)

I hate a liar
I'd set one on fire
they perjure the universe
turn everything around
till the worst is
applauded as the best and
the best kicked into the gutter
and spit on.

December 20, 1996

"I Am Enraged"—(a column like Ed Anger's):

The vile bestial settlers and sheep people wiped out the marsupial wolf.

Settlers need varmint like a cult needs enemies—and they [are] impervious to facts.

"Coyotes is decimated me lambs, me calves."

Absolute hogwash, of course.

Killed all the wolves and lynxes, so the deer overgrazed and starved.

Try beating sense into them—look at that face:

"How did you know it was about the wolf critter?"

"It sticks out all over you."

"Well they was killing our stock."

"No they weren't. Wild dogs—and how many was killed?"

"Well not so many."

"Exactly."

Slake this evil killing fever—stockmen need varmints like cultists need enemies.

Trucks unloading vicious, slobbering dogs:

"All right, turn 'em loose—kill, kill, kill."

Now dream of spilling pot seed on the floor, then putting into a picture where the seeds would stick.

December 21, 1996

What a bloody fool I was—unsung hero of a war with aliens nobody knew about (except the soldiers), and certainly would not want to hear about or believe now. And which "we" apparently lost.

In a dream an old bum told me:

"*We lost!*"

Remember David Edge for the British, wising me up about the CIA contingent:

"They order you to do things they are afraid to do themselves, *and then* laugh at you for doing it."

Remember the (enter T.P.)—the flying contraption I was on. Arch music laid on by Paul Bowles. Christopher Wanklyn was also there. I could feel the ship cracking up under me, just made it back on Pan music.

Paul said to Christopher:

"I was afraid it was going up."

"You mean the ship?"

"No, the whole planet."

Paranoid fantasies. Real enough at the time *and* in retrospect.

No, I wasn't hallucinating. "They" would like me to think I am—as Laurie Anderson says:

"THEY ARE."

Well, old unhappy far off things and battles long ago.

But the scars are still there.

Reversal:

"I'll take these into the art room," says the Butler.

"Certainly sir," says the titled master.

"Don't give me no shit, sir," says the Butler.

"Don't give me no shit," master interjects. "Sir?"

"Of course, you cocksucker . . ."—after long pause: "Sir."

December 22, 1996. Sunday

Gloomy Sunday. Last night no breakfast, in the Land of the Dead. Dave and Sue were there in hotel room sort of, and I see the time is 7:20 A.M.

Go down. A room with a long table and a photo of some vague food—meat? Vaguely red. Halfway up back wall is a large opening, I presume accesses the kitchen.

Now four striped gray cats come out. Then I see a black dude with a high starched white collar. Face like ceramic mask. I brace him for breakfast. He does not react.

From Paul Bowles:

"I disturbed an agitated centipede."

"Don't kill it."

"Someone should."

Why the hell not. To me it is the most abominable of all creatures.

What hideous dead-end led to the creation of a centipede? If you can't stand it, kill it!! With every other [animal] almost I say don't kill it: snakes, lizards, any decent life-form. But you're not a decent life-form anymore. Centipede legs is sprouting outa you.

"Get outa my bar. Quick. I don't like centipedes!"

Just a guess: Centipede came from a hot impasse. Scorpion crawls out cold—

maybe—well, a man has to play the cards he is dealt—

and who deals the cards?

"Making [it] just as hard as you can on the dealer."

Dealers change—his will is the wind's will.

Papa Hemingway said it:

"It just doesn't come anymore."

Your credit's gone Papa—your margin is et up.

Suicide is never good.

"It is a cowardly vetch, O my brothers."

How you doing, Burgess?

A writer should feel his way into all his fans everywhere, and fan them to action.

The whole evil of which the War Against Drugs is one factor. Mark it to its place: it's *EVIL* and it means no good for anything

Homo (experiment) Sap can or will create of value. It is here to exterminate.

For I shot a comrade sleeping
nine hundred of the hive, and
the swarm's disgrace.

Now they've halted it by a disposal unit on the ground.

"These are the unsightly tricks before high heaven, that make the Angels weep—"

When whales and seals and elephants weep, I cannot suppress the deadly Sin of Anger.

Always the cloth: "*Toro! Toro!*" and one charges again and again—

Let it go, like the men carried up by balloon ropes and couldn't get the thing in time to turn loose.

Brothers and Sisters, this sermon is about turning loose in time. Which means turning loose of all your body jerks—*clutch.* Too late. A hundred feet up.

Brothers and Sisters, turn loose while there is still a [milli] second of time.

Can a [milli]second take 3-D form?

A boy wished his brother dead, and his father in the package. When this wish emerged in his "life review," he said:

"I would rather sacrifice my own life."

And of course he meant it, but he didn't *feel* it. So he don't even get a whiff of grace.

In despair he threw himself somewhere, and was saved by his love for cats. No priest or psychiatrist could do it. It was Brion Gysin, *and:* "meow meow meow."

Is there any final honesty of character?

Not with the Other Half—sprawled through a man.

Yeah, men in sensory withdrawal often felt like "another body was slobbed across them."

Well, it sure was.

So take a good look at what is sprawled through you. Does it have your best interests in mind?

"Fuck no."

(Use them and lose them.)

December 23, 1996

(A boat in lake.) I was afraid it would turn over at high speed. Dreams less and less interesting.

December 24, 1996

With two boys. Jumped off cliff to show how one could float down. First jump-off-cliff dream in some time. Things are hotting up in L.O.D. No-breakfast dreams a few days ago.

So: How To Discover Past Lives.

Well, write one. Sure, I could write a batch, but easy:

Paris 1830 or so—Charles Baudelaire. Everything clear and sharp, the smell, the cats, the opium feel I know so well. I too had syphilis.

The horror. *Je m'y connais*—I know the sickness. It has come back.

The restaurants, cafés, the food, music—"*jet d'eau svelte parmi les marbres*"—Verlaine, Rimbaud, they run into each other—Paris—pissoir.

"*Simon, aime tu le bruit des pas, sur les feuilles mortes?*"

And this from a pissoir wall:

"*J'aime ces types vicieux, qu'ici montrent la bite.*"

"I like the vicious types who show the cock here."

Me too.

Back to Paris. So many *pharmacie*—

"*Codethyline Houdé?*"

"*Oui, Monsieur.*"

Verlaine: "an old faun in terra-cotta, foreseeing no doubt an unfortunate sequence (*une suite malheureuse*) to these hours that pass to the sound of tambourines."

I was never a King. An advisor—a Machiavelli—yes, but not the Prince.

I always had contempt for them. *They are stupid.*

Scribe, Priest, advisor, artist, yes.

Back deep are horrors that I cannot yet face. So we start with the easy ones like Paris.

Et puis? Well, Soldiers of Fortune in 1920—and earlier—doesn't hold water. *Just film.*

No smells, food, feeling. No gun really jumps in my hand. So where the—

December 26, 1996

The touchstone is a feeling of lyric joy.

A scene in a dream, intricate and large building, colors, water, two men talking. I find it in Conrad, in the banal reflections of Almayer on the unhealthy conditions on the east bank of the river.

I am there. The muddy river flows by—often the joy lasts only for a few seconds—

When people blather about "happiness," like some permanent medium you can accrete around yourself and never want for anything again. The archetype swindler's line.

"Greeve," in *The Heart of the Matter,* lists three types can be happy:

(1) The Unaware. Don't see. Won't see—some insulated with $$$.

(2) The Coarse. Hard, evil, like Bugsy Siegel—looks pretty well satisfied with himself, and a horrid sight it is, the ugliness bursting through—

"Bugsy!"

Two 30-30s in swelled head. What a sorry hero type to emulate.

Go in any Chicago bar. The clerks, the other loutish jerks, all trying to look like mobsters. Show me what they want to be, and I will tell you who they are: wretched failures at wretched jobs. Always, of course, "unfairly treated" by superiors.

Especially postal workers. Just yesterday another disgruntled mail carrier killed the supervisor—two shots in the head—

(all Postal Supervisors [should be] armed at all times)

Saturday, December 28, 1997.

Vague dreams.

Well, tried some exercises to uncover past lives. A few nibbles—a voice, a bit petulant and put-upon says:

"Well, I've been instructed to show you this."

And showed me very little.

The old Senseny house at Walton and Pershing. It was Mrs. Senseny who said of me:

"Stay away from it. It is a walking corpse."

Well, it isn't every corpse can walk. Hers can't.

And this walker can still talk.

(Hers can't, and this corpse can still walk.)

Oh well, not much light. I hope—about lives past or future or present to be found in this tawdry, snobbish, cruel—

How she could toy with a climbing Jewess:

"Oh, Mrs. Senseny, I had such fun at the Wallace party."

"You were *very* fortunate, *weren't* you."

The dining room was always cold and dank. The bedroom where she slept, and crept and leapt on some poor Jewess—the stink of it was pure Death. That is, it had no stink at all.

Don't know how I have such a clear picture of this room—and a blue kimono and blue coverlet, on untidy bed.

These are gloomy glimpses. Bits of vivid and, fortunately, vanishing details. The St. Louis bourgeois. . . .

"Well, I had a fine dinner, enjoyed it"—(after three stiff whiskeys)—"but I can't help feeling a twinge of conscience when I think of all the millions of people don't have enough to eat." (Discreet belch)

Dr. Senseny was a terrible doctor. Nearly killed me on a tonsil operation, flushed with an uneventful removal of adenoids, which I kept in alcohol in a jar next to a 6-inch centipede from under a rock in New Mexico, Valley Ranch, and my horse was named Grant. A Strawberry Roan. And the band played on. And I came near bleeding to death from his bungling hands.

"I did all I *could*," says he, and that was certainly no lie.

But I come of good stock and can survive the ineptitude of a socialite puff[ed]-shirt croaker (a sort of bladder with a face on it).

Cut his throat with my Scout knife and dragged him around the block behind my Red Bug three times.

"*He molested me!*" I sobbed.

And that was no lie, with his story about bringing a French fairy back to his digs. It was raining and cold:

"Then I knocked him into the gutter and slammed the door."
Yes, he sure was molesting me.

"Why if any son of mine, or any friend of mine, turned that way, I'd kill him with my own hands."

At this point I was molested, so I couldn't contain myself, kicked him in his nuts, and was on him with the shiv and all he could do was let out a squawk like a stricken turkey.

What all day? And so much negative Karma.

December 29?—30?, 1996

I was locked out of my apartment. The janitor with a pass key was Cabell Hardy on the 3rd floor.

(Found his letter today and immediately answered. Should have done before, but I did not register. The dream nudged me— *gracias* Allah.)

A little restaurant with one waitress. Somehow my gun was checked with her, and there were these two cops there (like Mexico). One had a harelip and looked like Big Al in the Beat Hotel (nostalgia hits me—the Beaux Arts Restaurant, the Balkan, Brion's room).

It is not certain they are or are not there to arrest me.

Outside is a dock (short and in ruins), deep blue water. Fish down there.

Reading *New Yorker* article about Hiroshima:

"Once, like everyone else, I thought the bomb had ended the war and saved many lives."

Include me out of your "everyone else." The war was already won. Japan was asking for peace through Sweden. It was obvious official USA were and are such shits as boggles a sane and relatively decent mind.

You see, they wanted a "virgin" target. Enough blood on that sheet to satisfy the bloody lot of you.

"Thank God it wasn't a dud," said Oppenheimer.

"We are become [Death], destroyer of worlds."

"Most perfect aiming point I've seen in this whole damn war," said Colonel Paul Tibbets, pilot of the (Ebola) *Enola Gay* that dropped it.

"Shadow left by a Japanese idler as he waited on the stone steps of a bank that never opened."

"Clock stopped at 8:15 A.M."

Gets worse and worse. The Ugly American keeps on getting uglier, until there is no uglier image what can be got.

And what is that final point? The ultimate F.U.?

Well now, of course you're a woman—I understand these things. I am a man of the world, my little short rib.

December 30, 1996

Reading *New Yorker*, July 31, 1995, account of "firestorms" in Hamburg occasioned by Allied bombing. (They don't need an Atom bomb.) Then Dresden, to break German morale. The result was history's second major firestorm. Like I say, top people in USA and England were such shits as you can't believe.

What is left in these minds? Very little of value to me or anyone I can relate to. "All my relations," as the Indians say. Like the drug anti's in Malaysia say: "dealers are not human to him."

And he—Mohathir Mohamed, Prime Minister—is not human to me. I curse him with my whole heart. There is nothing in him I feel for, or with.

Same goes for the firestorm impresarios.

So as this inglorious chapter in the USA draws to a dreary close with Clinton squeaking like the rat he turned out to be, that [in] Arizona and California together courts [are] quasi-legalizing marijuana for medical or any other purpose. . . .

You must mark it to its place. It is an *ILLEGAL* drug and by illegal, beyond question.

Tuesday, December 31, 1996.

I will start my auto—

you know—

If he—

Then I felt the touch of a higher power and I became a morphine addict. Best thing I ever did for myself. Without God's Own Medicine I could well have ended up one of those "Write the Great American Novel" [types] that never get off the ground, or an alcoholic academic:

"Will he get tenure? Will he break up with his lover of ten years?"

It is one tired soap opera and thanks to G.O.M. I didn't slip on it.

"Will he get tenure? Will the bank approve his application for a second mortgage? Should he make (risk) a pass at young Prescott, in violation of his own rule?"

He will write the Great American Novel someday, simply dripping with "high seriousness," that will pose and probe momentous questions.

In Egyptian hieroglyphs the idea of "question" is reeds and water.

The touch (nudge) of God's Own Medicine led me to *Junky,* [to] *Naked Lunch,* to finding a vacation—I mean, of course, *vocation.* A place in life. *My* place in life—and it opened my eyes to the evil that lurks behind the war against drugs. *Illegal* drugs. Not just any drugs. Once a drug becomes *illegal*, it acquires a sulfurous glow from the depths of Hell.

So through G.O.M. I gained self-respect—and in so doing, the respect of others.

I am an unabashed cultural Icon. I stand for the truth. I hate liars.

My familiar is the White Cat, formed of searing white moonlight under which all hidden plots, all lies and deceits, are brought to the light of The Hunting Cat. He can't be bought. Stack it to the ceiling. He can't be scared. He is light right through. Fear *is* deviousness. We march under the banner of The Hunting Cat.

What I mean by truth: I mean what is there when all the bullshit is gone. Not one lie left. All gone away.

And what, if anything, remains is TRUTH *and* consequences.

"I didn't mean—"

"Hell, I gotta big mouth, what would happen to me if I lost it—"

Good Old Boy. These are unsightly tricks.

"It has happened. You have lost it."

The day of the liar is done.

Truth is here when all the words are rubbed out. Words were made to lie with.

("I will go and laugh with my wife.")

Wherever that come from it was there.

Now, brothers and sisters, this is not done quick or easy. You find one lie in yourself and shove it out, and three more quicker than him come in. It's something you have to do every day, every hour, every second.

Trace down those lies. The White Cat will do the rest. The Hunting Cat.

We are—and by "we" I mean [we] who are sick of lies and bullshit—

Clinton—what a wrong number he turns out to be—won by default—better than Dole—says:

"There will be no RX's for illegal drugs like marijuana for medical or any other purposes."

An illegal drug is fucking illegal.

The whole Freudian Fraud was embraced by the upper middle ad[vertising and] pub[lishing] executives, because they knew they were compacted of lies. And they foolishly (fondly) thought some Yid from Frankurt-am-Main could straighten the whole mess out.

(Shoot a little G.O.M. and maybe the mess won't seem so messy.)

Remember Phil White saying about getting on junk:

"Worst thing can happen to a man."

Or he'd say:

"If God made anything better, He kept it for Himself."

Take no. 2:

I never regretted junk habit. Those lying bastards have the gall to ask me to speak about the evils of junk—I told them: "shallow pretext for police state," and they was off-line quick, lest they become contaminated by such evil dissent.

Well, Truth Party knows Evil when and where they see it.

"Talking is a woman."

Old, old song.

Any group—Black, Jew, woman, white, Arab, Chinese—that sets itself up as *the* superior creatures, end up as humorless (Communist) doctrinaire (atheists).

Any group puts out lying pamphlets like *Scab*—("We at *Scab*")
—are all "evil-hearted bores."

So who can prove that I didn't on my vacations go to Tangier
and rape children?

They got some of the rudiments of the Big Lie. But too far off
the mark.

It is not the truth that hurts, it is the outrageous lie.

If a man has spent years on a book, to fit it together like a sym-
phony, one says:

"This ill-conceived so-called novel, obviously slopped together
in a few weeks, has no serious claims even to criticism."

That's what gets a writer's Angora goat. "Why have I spent
seven years on [this] book—"

"slopped together"—

What we are up against: liars with no honesty or integrity or
decency, just plain bastards, like the people try to run down squir-
rels or cats or Gila monsters (an endangered species) or cut up
manatees with their speed boats:

"Ha Ha Ha."

January 4, 1997

Just reading Hersey, and other Hiroshima accounts, and got mad
as Ed Anger in *The* [*Weekly World*] *News* again.

That lying bastard Conant of Harvard defends dropping the
bomb. In his tendentious article he does not even mention radiation sickness: "the Atomic Plague."

Scene: Conant at podium, all seems very decorous very, very
Harvard, then . . .

"Mr. Conant, you don't mention radiation sickness in your
article? Were you aware of this syndrome when you wrote the
article in question?"

All over the hall, voices:

"Yes did he know about . . ."

And someone has smuggled in a magic lantern, projecting horrible burns.

"No, he didn't know about nothing."

Conant visibly reels. He is not accustomed to such treatment.

"Well it was a short article—I could hardly be expected—"

Voice:

"He could *hardly* be *expected*—"

Shrill, piercing voices:

"And you knew nothing of Japanese overtures for surrender?" . . .

Voices:

"He knew nothing. . . . He was a *good* nigger, knew his place and kept in it."

"Good nigger . . ."

"Knew his place . . ."

These voices dispersed through the audience, suddenly burst like a bomb in waves of sound—five hundred tape recorders— five hundred voices:

"Get off the stage!"

"Lying cocksucker!"

"*Crawl off the stage!* Don't want your type in here!"

"Boo! Boo! Hiss! Hiss!"

Vain attempts to restore order. Conant hustled out by security, pelted with rotten eggs and tomatoes—in a state of collapse.

January 7, 1997

Memoirs—what you wouldn't want anyone to know.

"My past was an evil river—*une fleuve maudit.*"

Without tenure—who wants an unemployed teacher of Creative Writing.

So write: the law is Love.

In simple form: a *feeling* for.

Par exemple, I feel no feeling for a centipede. For an abandoned kitten, I feel much sympathy.

Where did the centipede come from?

And what betrayal of the human species could have led some sonofabitch to feed live baby mice to a caged centipede?

Centipede—come from very hot place, from very hot place which formed the centipede . . . the *OVENS*, the *Ovens*, the *Oooovens* . . .

Well, forget [it], who cares anymore.

As Sri Aurobindo said: "It is all over."

January 8, 1997. Wednesday

Another dream of going through Customs with drugs or guns. Definite fear of arrest and imprisonment.

Walking by marble statues, mutilated—a finger here, a prick there.

I hope tomorrow I will be in a luxury or decent hotel, *not* in a jail cell.

Strong feel of *combat*. Get up and fight or Die.

Lying bastards from some do-what-we-tell-you orders: "Cannabis is harmful."

Got some Albanian expert up his sleeve:

"Yes, we consider use of this *illegal drug* as *proof* of insanity."

January 10, 1997. Friday
THE WHITE CAT.

Advert—[*Lawrence*] *J*[*ournal*] *World*:

"Free to good home. White cat. 2530 Rosebud Lane. tele 555-0676."

I called. I went. 3 P.M. Sunday. Woman (Sally?) very nice, looks oriental.

Beautiful cat. I took it home. Locked in front guest room. The cat—"Marigay"—Sanskrit for White Cat—screamed and threw himself against the door.

Today—Friday, Jan 9, 10?—Roger Holden agreed to take the cat. He will stay over weekend at Bradley's Vet Hospital.

I could not stand two more days (no sleep last night).

Why so upset? Don't know. Listening to his cries, I was struck by such a feeling of dread and depression [as] I have never experienced before. Why?

Board members, bosses, dictators, bankers, crawl under their desks screaming:

"The White Cat! The White Cat!"

Old lives from nowhere. Old quotes from somewhere.

The White Cat—under his searing light all hidden things come to light. He is the "tracker," the hunter who follows the track or scent.

All over the world, millions of cats are crying to be let in, or out, crying until they give up finally, and I get a few hours of rest.

Like now Marigay the White Cat is gone I can shut my ears to suffering, hungry, cold, homeless cats? I couldn't stand another night.

So investigator, hunter, follower of the track?

Nothing covers the feeling of foreboding and dread I felt to [hear] those cries, just plain cat cries. A willful young tomcat. So?

"The whiteness of the cat."

The White Cat (under the breakfast table in Algiers, Louisiana, across the river from New Orleans and into the trees).

Is this simply a foreboding of death. My death? Felt like someone else's. Hope not.

Depression lifts with a spot of vodka and prospect of a quiet night.

We are not getting to The White Cat. I see the cat vivid as a 3-D image. I love the cat. I receive his searing White Light. No pretense or lies to conceal.

As to pressure to Lie—I elect to fight.

Go!

I invoke: rows of naked red male forms moving forward in a definite pattern—a killing fan-out:

Kill! Kill! Kill!

Like we used to kill.

The pure killing purpose.

Now? Turned out to pasture like old horses, is it?

Well, I got one good kick left.

January 11, 1997. Saturday

State of the Union? Wretched beyond belief. A million dollars to study medical uses for Cannabis!

I could save them the money: [relieves] glaucoma, stimulates appetite and suppresses nausea in late morphine withdrawal, or in chemotherapy. A general tonic with no side effects. A reliable aphrodisiac—there if you want it. Doesn't embarrass you by an untimely erection, like [while] meeting the Queen or other dignitary.

(What a ploy to disgrace an enemy or diplomat on the podium.)

Cannabis always under control. In short, a gamut of uses.

If [the] report is favorable [it] will, of course, be suppressed—like the Porno. report under Nixon, who said Leary was "the most dangerous man in America"—dangerous to lying bastards like Nixon, and Bush and Reagan and—

"oft fold dreary etcetera to bed."

Will lie in its sleep.

So why the foreboding about the White Cat?

Perhaps—future—snow white.

L. Ron Hubbard appears in a dream, his face with a deep space tan. We will head a streamlined Scientology takeover. He is dressed in what looks like deep-sea-fishing, certainly nautical, garb.

Well, why not give it a glim? Recall he was human, then he wasn't:

"I am not from this planet, but I got the best intentions."

Sure, sure, we all do.

"How papers slither away."

At this point paper with White Cat info slipped to the floor—at breakfast—now at 4:50 P.M. find paper on floor.

The White Cat is really charged hot here. Something *bad*.

American Narcotics—"*bad*," says Dr. Dent. Evil, I say.

And so many power-freak agents would roll in it like a dog rolls in carrion, *and* grunt, *and* squeal:

"I am *right*."

I don't stink so.

(Jim here now.)

The issue open? Reeds in water.

The investigator, follower of the track, moon cat, white light cat, Cleanser of the Darkness, the night—

So?

Chain of Evidence falls into the Waste Basket. (Why capitalized?)

"William Burroughs, is it?"

—Ridley Pearson.

So I into waste basket?

The Son of Sam—Samson.

January 12, 1997. Sunday

Dreaming of insects, according to *The News,* may presage a deadly illness.

(*Peut etre . . . qui vivre verra.*)

Last night a quarter, *barrio* of rot, falling-down wood houses, crawling with roaches and flies. It seems that I have a "cottage" here, called "the May Cottage." I reflect I would have to move in with pounds of insecticide, pyrethrum perhaps.

I notice the *barrio* is not large and quite square, and that the infestation of insects is confined to this space (obviously transported, but separate from its environs).

What else?

I have had many dreams of stinging flies. Connected to Paul Bowles:

"We must never allow anyone to leave this planet!"

(Paul in state of collapse.)

"Off the track! Off the track! Just no hope at all."

I see Paul's face quite clear, out there in the snow, zero Fahrenheit.

". . . To think how they must *ache* in icy hoods and mail."

Keats, "St. Agnes' Eve."

"They'll have swift steeds that follow—"

Fantasy of running a roadblock. I have this fantasy on the way to Kansas City, Thursday. I am a bit junk sick.

Paul Bowles caught the junk feel in "Mr. Young and Mr. Woo," a short story. Usually a nonuser is way off, like *The Man With the Golden Arm*—Algren. He didn't know the first thing about junk. Later, I hear, admitting his ignorance.

"A snitch in time saves a dime"—rhyme.

So what does suburban Kansas say to me?

It says: "Kill!"

So I can see it. Get the dead off my sight.

"Bring out your dead!"

And give the Driver some head.

New moon in the pale blue, like a sliver of white nail. A little silver sliver of a moon in the blue plate of sky.

Why? Like nothing anywhere.

Where it was all—

St. Patrick:

"I saw the old moon with the new moon in its eyes."

What is it that shines from the eyes of an atheist when he says: "When I die, I will be all the way dead"? Like it gives them some special grinning satisfaction?

January 13, 1997. Monday

There was some large insect under my sheets, like a large spider—and scorpion—turned back sheets and could not find it.

I was junk sick. Looking for a little codeine. Anything.

Talking to mother on phone—

Was it always so? We are the only enlightened, illuminated to realize that you never give opiates for a cold? That dealers deserve the death penalty?

What a lying, stupid bore—the war on drugs.

They even had the gall to ask me to speak or write in support. My refusal was definitive.

Out to feed the fish. All the places where Spooner used to be hit me with a physical impact. The cat was part of myself. He died October 4, Friday, 1996.

"Sorry he didn't make it," the vet says.

I *knew* when I held him in my lap he was dying—then he jumped down and pissed under the table.

The White Cat is now with Roger Holden. A good home.

Why the feeling of dread?

(I think I forestalled some disaster, like the cat getting out, can't find, etc.)

Who will ever know what misfortunes were aborted.

Or could be in the future, or refer to my own precarious state of health.

January 14, 1997. Tuesday

Reading a bio of Francis Bacon by Dan Farson. Years ago, [Farson] organized a TV show for me and Alex Trocchi.

Francis calls attention to some graffiti, and I claim the all-time best from one of those outdoor pissoirs in Paris:

"*J'aime ces types vicieux
qu'ici montrent la bite.*"

"I like the vicious types
who show the cock here."

"Oh oh, whoo hoo, me too!"

Quote from an out-of-print, out-of-mind gay novel. I heard the writer killed himself. It was very good. Can't even recall the title or the writer's name. It was [McGary] or something vaguely Irish.

Another lost MS. Scenes of the novel pass through my screen, the little "whoo hoo" queen. Another twisted nasty queer who worked in a government seamen's employment agency. Another: "He had never seen a youth as aware of his blood, and—"

"There was a little dog named Rover
    and when he was dead he was dead all over."
    "*You* know!"
    Many years later I questioned Ted [about] the "all-over" po-
sition, and he snarled, suddenly and out of character, unchar-
acteristically—said—snarled—snapped, the real Mort:
    "You *know!*"

Dreams full of cats and dogs.
    I ask a female attendant: "What color cat?"
    She says: "Nut brown."
    Many cats, some of a *rich* nut brown color. Such cats. Both
cats and dogs in the dream.

January 15, 1997. Wednesday

Favorite quotes:
    "J'aime ces types vicieux
    qu'ici montrent la bite"
    On wall of outdoor pissoir in Paris.
    "*Simon, aime tu le bruit des pas sur les feuilles mortes?*"—Remy
de Gourmont.
    "Magic casements opening on the foam
    of perilous seas in fairy lands forlorn."—Keats.
    "Un vieux faun en terre cuite
    presageant, sans doute, une suite
    malheureuse a ces heures
    dont la suite tour a son des tambours"
    —Paul Verlaine.

"An old faun in terra-cotta foreseeing, doubtless, an unhappy end to these hours, of which the passing turns to the sound of tambourines."

Difficult to express the "sound" of silent hand drums, which is the magic of this poem.

Verlaine is certainly one of the greatest of pure lyric form:

"La calme clair de lune, triste et beau, qui fait revez les oiseux dans l'arches. Et sanglot d'extase les jets d'eau suite parmis les marbres."

"These our actors, as I foretold you, were all spirits and are melted into air—into thin air; even so the gorgeous palaces, the cloud-topped towers, the great globe itself—this insubstantial pageant faded leaves not a wrack behind."

January 17, 1997. Friday

Another immortal quote. Chinese pushers in the 1920s found white customers so unreliable and prone to inform that when approached by a Caucasian, [they] would say:

"No glot. Clom Fliday."

"I may be old. But I'm still desirable."

(That was 50 years ago. Are his bones still desirable?)

"What is it in a man's blood that makes him like that?"

—About a queer bullfighter who let his mother's grave rent run out, and she is dug up and thrown in the common bone pit.

The defeated General does a strip tease with his medals, and braids the lot while he says:

"It costs more than I can pay."

"I surrender, dear."

By now he is stark naked with an obsequious hard-on.

Piecing life together is like jigsaw puzzle.

Whose biographer could I be? Only one person. Brion Gysin.
Well, get in touch with Geiger. Get on it.
My past.

January 17, 1997

Beat Hotel. Room 32. The cure. The *Life-Time* people. Snell and
Dean. The aliens have *no solid waste*.

Snell sent me a note:

"'Hey boy, check my bags!' Laying bare his scrotum at Bitch
Box 69."

"If you want it, *it's all urine*."

The price too heavy?

Anyhoo, I didn't buy.

Can I bring it back, the magic and danger and fear of those
years in 9 rue Git-le-Coeur and London and Tangier—the magic
photographs and films—

Did shake them up a bit. One theater manager said he had
never had so many snarling complaints, or so many congrats from
the heart, or seen so many objects forgotten on seats—cameras,
umbrellas, purses (usually empty), hats, etc.

Day after day the movie was flickering:

"Towers, Open Fire."

In Tangier John Hopkins visits me in the Lottery Building.
He says:

"Smells like a sea war in here."

Yes, and the time in the Muniriya, I had [overdosed], and just
made it to my room. Okay in five minutes.

Almost death so many times—in the bar at Hotel Chelsea,
Robert Filliou asked me:

"How many times did they try to kill you?"

Brion kept me on track:

"Just pretend you are not being attacked."

Difficult at times. There was a feeling of gray despair, sudden glimpses of hope.

It's a long way to Tipperary—99 Cromwell Road, where I took the Apomorphine cure with Dr. Dent.

Kicking in room 15. Ian Sommerville. (I hear an elevator.) (T.P. is here to make dinner.)

"Old unhappy
far off things
and battles
long ago."

One of Mikey's black lovers in Tangier said:

"It is terrible—Spirits fighting."

"Day after day the war."

Day after day the bore of war that wears you down—isn't that a war of attrition?

January 18, 1997. Saturday

I've only scratched the surface here. The up feeling of immortality, and power. The down—"it is down in my soul for the gray despair"—vast clinics of terminals, stretching into gray distance, hazy and meaningless— No hope.

In a dream an old bum said (this was 1965, I was living at the Chelsea):

"We lost!"

Did we? I'm ready to hit it again.

So where.

The Pan Rites of Joujouka—a boy danced in front of me for a few seconds—impersonal as Pan, God of nature.

Did Pan die when Christ was born? No. But he took a beating—some wavy broken glass appeared on the trampled earth where the boys were dancing.

And I got a glare of hate from the Green Nun—sitting there in Arab drag—

Brion Gysin is the only man I have ever respected. Others I have liked, admired. . . .

What then is the meaning of respect? When all lies, deceit, pretense is stripped away, what remains? The truth of a painting, or a book or a man.

No one is perfect.

No, but by the flaws in the picture the truth will emerge.

Any[way]—last night, vague dream I was somewhere, couldn't stay long—I packed laundry sack with drawstring . . .

What else?

The lake, a Moroccan, Jewish, German slum.

So I must let everything all the way in, a vast wind to blow everything that doesn't belong away.

(I am transparent.)

January 21, 1997

"Jan. 21, 1997. Last words in this diary of William S. Burroughs."

Just reading the life of Francis Bacon, his horrible behavior at times—he *booed* and *hissed* the singing of Princess Margaret, in a private house—

On another occasion:

"There was no charm that afternoon, instead he (Francis) descended to the foulest obscenity."

Gilbert and George said:

"But don't you see? That's how Bacon is. He is absolutely right to behave as he wants."

Not as he wants. As he *has to* behave.

An artist must be open to the muse. The greater the artist, the more he is open to "cosmic currents." He *has to* behave as he does. If he has "the courage to be an artist," he is *committed* to behave as the mood possesses him.

"That's the man who booed Princess Margaret!"

—the peasantry shrink back from his sulfurous glow.

Two bad nights with my *hiatus*—the Chinese food took a heavy toll of my guts, could hardly wait for dawn and methadone. Maybe a little codeine. A "pinkies" packet left, so I think . . . No. Well, who can blame an addict's fingers?

In my life review I hate so many [that] I should have put in their place *then,* and put them there *now.*

What a waste of one-upmanship on the long-dead (likely), or certainly inaccessible.

The price an artist pays for doing what he wants is that he *has to do it.*

I was asked:

"Why did you stop writing?"

I would not know any more than I would know why I started writing.

Try not to be as obtuse as you are.

I wait for dawn
    and 60 milligrams of methadone.
    Of course I could cheat
    but as the con dick told me:
    "You get away with it

twenty years, you're only kidding
yourself."
—and who else is worth kidding?

Waiting for dawn
    and my methadone
    to fit the pieces
    into the resident beasties.

So?
    "He (Francis) played roulette and he had some good wins."
    "It happens. The only way to win at the horses, is to never start
to win."
    Plunge when you are winning.
    fold when you are losing.
    That's the law.
    Why bother?—
    It's a full-time job, and for me, not worth the energy.

January 22, 1997. Wednesday

Vivid color dream last night:
    I come to a road junction. I turn right. A street with pine trees
and a rural aspect. Buildings—in one window, a de-barked sec-
tion of tree shellacked. Nature-genre sculpture, I presume. At end
of street some top-heavy-looking buildings.
    I am looking for a drugstore to buy paregoric. None on this street.
    I get in plane with someone and we take off flying low to ex-
plore the left side of junction, which is a large city with huge build-

ings. One is a large square edifice from which rises a square tower in glazed yellow brick, about a hundred feet tall. Other towering constructions in red and yellow and russet, very spectacular.

I comment on this to an old woman, who looks on-the-nod. She says:

"Yes I've seen it often."

I ask where I can find a drugstore. She says:

"Right here."

And there is my bottle of paregoric with an old-style cork stopper—two ounces.

The store is divided by a colored screen and is very large. Whole city very sci-fi. Like nothing on earth.

January 24, 1997. Friday

"Across the river, and into the trees
    Over the hills and far away"

Man sent his servant to the market to buy bread. Servant returned, white [with] fear and said:

"I saw Death in the market and he made a threatening gesture."

The servant saddled his horse, gassed his car, mounted his motorcycle and rushed posthaste to Samarra.

Later the man went to the market and met Death.

"Why," he asked, "did you frighten my servant with a threatening gesture?"

Death answered:

"It was not a threatening gesture. It was a gesture of surprise to see him here, since I have an appointment with him in Samarra."

A friend underwent a period of deep depression, during which every failure, humiliation was played back to him.

Now what could do that? Obviously a parasitic *being*.

All the psychiatrists have been looking in the wrong places, the wrong direction. No wonder they are not getting results. Demonic or disadvantageous possession is more to the point. Which they will never see, being themselves possessed.

I was sort of arrested by Shen, I mean, Shein & O'Grady, who actually arrested me fifty years ago, more or less. (When you see a Jew can an Irishman be far behind?) Just cops. Trying to be as nice as they aren't. No push. No slap. Just a few snarls from Shein:

"Now don't get any ideas about running, Burroughs."

I didn't have any ideas like that. Violation of Public Health Law 334—Obtaining narcotics by the use of fraud.

O'Grady explained to the booking sergeant that [it] was not a felony but a misdemeanor. He was a nice guy basically, like the Irish cop in New Orleans:

"Oh well, it's just our job to arrest them, and there's no hard feelings—just that's the way it is."

I know the role he plays—he's the old doctor. That's his profession.

"Here comes the old doctor."

"Here [comes] the Japanese sandman."

"Dead Man Blues"—

"Just an old secondhand man,
trading new dreams for old."

The old cop routine: nice cop—tough cop. Con cop—tough cop. It still works. Old, old act.

"Now look, why don't you make it easy on yourself—and on us, too. We don't like violence."

These are archetypical experiences, like being in jail. Five times, me. It gives you a basic feeling.

Oh yes, I'd forgotten four months in the Army. That is jail time. Where you can't get out. Whole fucking planet is jail time.

And Bellevue and Payne Whitney. Any place you can't get out of is jail.

Like the Universe? Maybe?

What is outside the expanding universe? The final horror? Nothing.

A cat plays with the edge of my Hudson Bay blanket.

They wanted more and more people to work in their factories, mines and mills to buy the products so made. Now a majority of such great stupidity and such barbarous, bigoted manners threatens us all.

A selective pestilence seems the only remedy to a situation always more hopeless.

A priest said:

"We may just have to start over."

He was informed about the atrocities in Africa, the Hutu and the Tutsi—the rampant intertribal violence, massacres.

January 25, 1997. Saturday

I must tell James:

Please never conceal from me any nasty letters or reviews. I want the names of these creeps. The addresses, so I can put one of my curses on them. It will give me something to do.

And jog a few higher-up elbows hiding behind [the] nameless assholes. I will make a list and cross names off one after another.

Like the new rich in St. Louis. At his daughter's coming-out party. *Nobody showed*. She went mad. He made a list of all the invitees who didn't show. And ruined them one after another. It gave meaning to his life. He crossed off the last name on his death-bed, gave a contented belch and died. He was a fully fulfilled evil old man.

I've a weakness for evil old men.

"Cactus Jack"—described by Lewis as a "whiskey-drinking poker-playing evil old man."

And a KGB General, described as "this evil old man"—he bruised his shoulder shouting "traitors and incompetents" in the old days, and when the KGB came into being, he was already there. This evil old man.

The Mafia had some good ones, like "Fat Tony" Salerno. He was an authentic evil old man. Died in prison at 80—with scores of bones under his truss. He didn't trust doctors. Evil old men have these obsessions—endearing, you know, shows they are human.

So many stories I don't want ever to write. They might come true!

A potentate who would summon writers, artists known to be amusing, diverting and say:

"Amuse me. When you cease to amuse me, you will die—some quick and easy, who have after all provided *some* amusement—others, slow and painful, for boredom inflated."

(How dull!!!)

Be there a man
    with soul so dead
    never to himself

has said
"My God I acted
like an absolute
shit !" and then
then and then—fold
bitter etcetera to bed

"His life review will be heavy."

"Do not corrupt Allah's WILL, dreading thy actions done."

Or *worse: denying* thy actions done.

None so hopelessly blind as he who will not *look*.

The searing light of The White Cat brings old lies and hidden things to pitiless disclosure and light.

You see, if things went completely *wrong*, I would have no alternative. I would leap for the throat, with the claws we have lost in the evolutionary game.

Like the old "just try and shake your head 60 trillion years from now."

—Of the species addressed, about half are now extinct.

The mechanics, technicians there, turning out molds.

"Look at this. A venomous flying lizard, got jet propulsion— and here's one can live four hundred years, and and and . . ."

January 26, 1997. Sunday

Getting older I find the whole explicit subject of sex appalls me.

This was brought home to me when I read "A Visit to Priapus" by the writer whose name I cannot remember. Writer goes up into the lobster coast to meet with this boy who has a tremendous cock.

"You wouldn't *believe* it, my dear."

Nor do I want to, as the story unfolded with writer eating lobster after crab and this—to me—already totally repulsive youth grinning idiotically over the lobster, which was in itself becoming always more repulsive.

All right.

Quelle horreur—like some hideous deformity of the genitals.

It wasn't till next morning that "Priapus spent," while the writer spent himself twice.

What was his name. He's dead now.

I'm told [he] always referred to me as "that terrible man." Never met me, of course, but I take on mythological significance in certain blinkered views.

He wrote *An Apartment in Athens*, which I read. Vague notion he wrote family farm sagas in Wisconsin. Full-bodied. Knew Somerset Maugham. (I think he, too, would say: "terrible man.")

The nameless one living on his brother's estate in a tenant farmer's cottage, tastefully done over into real American Gothic, with spinning wheels that don't spin, grandfather clock that's stopped dead, never to go again.

When the old man died—or was pushed.

And a cream separator in my own kitchen, my brain reels at the thought, and butter churns and ice-cream freezers, old salt-and-ice things.

I can be as bitchy as any queen from "the biggest closet in the Mediterranean"—the Villa Mauresque.

I still don't got his name. I have the feeling it has been *physically* removed.

Like to make an anthology of my favorite passages in books: Céline, the scene on the boat to Africa where he talks his way out of a beating:

"All this time I felt my self-respect slipping away from me and finally—as it were—*officially* removed."

In Conrad: Captain Marlowe talks to French naval officer who traveled in the Patna:

"As to what life may be worth when the honor is gone?"

Lord Jim: interview between Councillor Mikulin and [Razumov], the protagonist. Catches sight of his face in the mirror next day:

"It was the most unhappy face he had ever seen."

Looking for that name, lurking behind a deformed penis like some tuberous plant, getting always bigger and bigger—and oozing semen never spurting—oozing something fibrous, like bark. Old rotten, greasy bark—disgust me to see it.

So?

Names. Names and addresses.

Hot cop breath in his face. He throws back his head and sings in Chinese falsetto:

"Miranda when day is done I hear your call

Miranda, we meet beside the water

Miranda you're just a name to me

Miranda? I hear your call—"

(cups hand to his ear)

Basta. What is his bloody fucking *name.* Westcoat? Something like. He putters around. Can't write.

"Anyone talks about why he don't write, he turns his back and walks away." —Ted Morgan.

West coast harts field.

Why do you hide your name from me?

Because I hate you.

Why?

Because you . . .

Why.

You slop it up.

Hemingway said:

"It don't come anymore."

So where did it go?

Oh well, out with "wind and the trees and his mother's bones."

This gets us no closer to his name.

In a gazebo, a summer house. Ted Morgan describes an encounter between Maugham and this nameless one. Apparently Maugham opened his dressing gown (he, too, was a guest in this rather commodious cottage): "to reveal quite a respectable phallus."

Tee hee hee, Priapus.

Well So-and-so, if you call me a terrible man, I shall do what I can not to disappoint you. What is *your* name, you who dare call me a terrible man?

He's dead now. Like so many other wise guys who wouldn't tell me their fucking names. I am a nice guy, but there are limits. Easy way and a tough way to do things.

Perhaps [why] I am so uniquely terrible is simply that I represent total Dissent. Total Dissent. T.D. 19 + 4 = 23.

Total exposure of dual human structure, which will entail *basic biologic changes* of the human species.

(It is laughable.)

"*Qui vivre verra.*"

Who lives will see.

"Your name, sir?"

Well now, let's try and fit the pieces back together into some being with some survival potential.

OK. Light, Action Camera:

"What are you doing on this set? My set?

"Well, I've got my orders."

"Name?"

Consulted the index in Morgan's *Maugham*. A real job. Best thing Ted ever did. And I got that name:

Glenway Wescott.

The "dirty thirties" as the Scientologists call them. Don't know why.

What the hell is auditing? Listening to trauma *and passing it on.*

Here is one revolting process: look at someone on the street, and imagine everything that is wrong with *you* is *wrong with him or her.*

(Unburden that whole load of shit on some passerby. May encounter a tough one, catches on straightaway and throws it back with intent and interest.)

See what I mean?

I sure do see exactly what you mean—imagine every disgusting and abject thing about someone sitting opposite in the subway, bus—or nail one down walking. See his shoulders droop, look at that look of shame on an Assistant Professor, as vile images flood his brain.

(There is no doubt about it: Scientology is evil and basically ill-intentioned and nasty.)

So now at last I have the name: Glenway Wescott. Old American stock.

"Miranda, unhanda me."

"Wo is das Wurm? Siegfried?"

"Up your ass you old nance?"

"How dare you affront a great artist?"

"Artist is it? Brown artist? assfuck *artiste*—"

"I will not be drawn into a fish wife screamer."

Meanwhile the S.C.I. has sat back with a contented belch, and when The White Cat brought in the searing light of truth that obliterated the lie—

The name from Ted Morgan's bio of Maugham:
Glenway Wescott
Glenway Wescott
"Glenway Wescott—Who were you?"
Copains shouting at each other.

He was reading it as his spirits hit the toilet.

Careful, maybe not who he seems not to be.

Receive M with open arms if you want it that way.

"Kill" Q on request.

He's good people.

Insults, years ago, are nourished in the present. Cut off present source.

Where were we when we weren't there?

Oh yes.

We are at the entrance to the 18 Maze. Here time has little or much influence. A million years can pass in an injection, an orgasm, a glimpse of "pure lyric happiness" (Paul Bowles).

The rules of the Maze are transient, and guidebooks always suspect to carrying terrible ruled-out cons.

Harry Phipps on the line:

"Watch it William. Watch it all the time."

"I was sorry to hear of your untimely death. My deepest sympathy. O.D. on coke ampules. Must have been nasty."

"It was—one of my worst. Error had me."

January 29, 1997. Wednesday

Fletch is getting old and cranky. Rarely purrs for me anymore.

Yes, he displaced Ruski. I am sure there is a lesson there, as there is at every turn, another lesson to learn and always too late.

If only I had known then what I know now, which may well have saved many an aborted misfortune.

Quite literally —abortion is murder. I would have none of it. Used those very words. Joan would have been willing.

When I drove Joan to the hospital, instead of waiting around biting my nails like a cartoon husband, [I] went back to my jeep, probably to get a nip, and somebody had left a puppy in my jeep. It was whining and barking.

A lesson there. After which I can never leave an animal as I once did.

The Tangier cat that caught meat in his paws.

More painful life review.

The things I had to do to do the things I had to do.

I sound like some tiresome old mean typhoon—I mean tycoon, of course, mulling over all the people he trampled down, like the bloody horse's ass he was.

And I was obsessed, possessed by writing, after a late start at thirty-five with *Junky*.

Forgot about the cat that caught food in its paws. Forgot about Mother and Dad, Joan and Billy. I had to keep moving, New York—

Once when I left Palm Beach, Billy said, age nine or ten:

"I knew he'd just go back to New York."

Back to junk, and what I had to learn, to do what I did.

Basta for now.

I see old man Getty in his big armchair with his *vicuña* shawl around his old dying bones.

He believed in reincarnation and was afraid he might be re-borned as a Coolie, lugging barrels of oil to the tankers.

"Wake up, Wong. We're on shift."

And know what he read?

"Clive *of* India" or *in* India, for the chrissakes.

He was an artist at the long-distance phone. Never went to any of these places in Arabia. Did it all from a suite in the George Cinq in Paris.

"He was an individual."

I got that from a bartender where I was briefly, and inappropriately, also a bartender, how this detective beat him up and he caught the cop later with two friends—took his gun and handed bartender/protagonist a black jack from the dick—(little pocket for it):

"No. I don't need it."

"Did he put up much of a fight?" I asked.

"He was an individual."

"My past was an evil river." Verlaine.

"The moving finger writes and having writ, moves on. Nor all your assets can call that finger back to cancel half a line. Nor all your tears wash out a word of it."

Grief is a basic emotion, like joy and war—the pure killing purpose. I have known them all.

And all this I owe to one man—Brion Gysin. The only man I have ever respected.

"How many times did they try to kill you?"

Robert Filliou of the Domaine Poetique speaking, in the bar of the Chelsea, 222 [W.] 23rd Street.

During the war. Day after day I had to get this article, this letter off. The heat they could turn on. I'd had so many exposures to that withering heat.

All war stories get dull and pompous in the telling.

We had to retreat—so many times. And we came back maimed. Whole areas of thought and feeling burned out.

Remember in the Minzah Hotel, Tangier. I'd ordered dinner and wine, when the heat ray hit me. I stood up slowly, up one flight—thank Allah—some cold water [on] my face, came back down and ate dinner.

Wonder what casualties the others suffered?

Remember Mikey's black lover, who was psychic, said:

"It is terrible here. Spirits fighting."

Indeed they were, and then Leary breezed in with mushrooms.

Back to the Beat Hotel, 9 rue Git-le-Coeur:

Brion's amazing face changes. . . . Once he addressed me with his incomparable charm:

"Charles Baudelaire."

And Baudelaire was in the room, and a Prince who lived in black fear of assassination, quivering, shying like a horse from a barrage of danger—

And always the fear, like pain, drags you down—fear of jail, fear of poverty—four noble truths.

I am called to the U.S. Embassy and shunted to some narcotics official, who says the French are getting ready to deport me.

"I'd just heard this on the spirit line."

My lawyer, [Maître] Bumsell, makes inquiries and says:

"Nothing to it."

For some reason in some obscure plan, I am being routed back to the States.

Like I say, war stories are dull, blunted, [like] you come out of it.

Remember when I was at 77 Franklin St. in the 70s, and this fan from Kentucky breezed in and said that as he was coming in from the airport in a taxi, a voice in his head kept saying:

"You have to kill him."

He didn't.

Got this anthology of cat horror, *Twists of the Tale*, edited by Ellen Datlow—yes, she stooped dat low—and (I've forgotten the correct [title]) "The Cat From Hell," by Stephen King, is a hoot.

You see, an autobio must be a jumble of fragments.

Start.

I stood in front of the mirror on the landing, in the eerie medium of childhood that withers away under time, and said to the image:

"Three."

It was my third birthday, and on from there always the feel of something terrible just under the surface—like the horrible dream in a smell of coal gas when I was eating my mother's back, and she screamed she'd had the dream. I was leaning over from the front and eating her back.

So take this to your priest, Father Murphy?

"Well, I don't think you should dwell on these matters, it can become unwholesome. Just say a few Hail Mary's and go on about your business and mine."

The Catholic church has become completely unspiritual.

See, see where G.O.M. streams in the hydro-morphine at dawn on pain-ravaged flesh, pain-riddled flesh, not getting enough G.O.M.

January 29, 1997. Wednesday

Bad night. Much pain in gut.

In dream I said to someone—Mother?—

"I must go to a hospital."

Just read a story by Walter de la Mare—jolly good.

How evil can an evil old bastard get?

Well, "this evil old recluse"—now, it isn't easy to be evil in a vacuum. Oh sure, his Will, hate of his sisters and everybody.

But what does an evil old recluse *do?* Just sit and be evil?

Very difficult, unless one is an adept at evil and a *made man,* got all the medals.

That is why this is such a good story of evil. Very *special* evil. He'd been stewing in it for twenty years, in "this vile, jaded, forsaken house."

Walter in bed there, by the evil old recluse himself.

The almost total absence of any goodness in the human spirit condemns the heart to an appalling isolation?

Walter was led there to write the story, led by a character in the story he was going to write.

Here is this evil old recluse, stewing in his evil, year after year, in a vile, jaded, forsaken house.

How evil can one get under such circumstances?

Leave your money to the to-be-set-up Brutality Dept. of Scotland Yard.

He did leave it, all the Pounds to Scotland Yard to aid in persecuting and prosecuting all malefactors, miscreants and dregs in society to the limit of the law and beyond, if some technicality obstruct the wheels of justice. Writing letters to *The Times* occupied a good portion of his time.

At this point fate seemed to put a royal flush into his hand. A "sensitive" had detected strong "pure currents." Soon she had enrolled a potent battery.

Handle with caution. It's *HOT.*

Hot hate on the half-shell.

Yes, an Evil Recluse is in a class by himself by definition. His food is sent up by dumbwaiter?

Well, she recruits him, and they set up a station in Topeka and put out a world of hurt.

Sure, sure but for how long and to what purpose?

Here I sit with my three old cats, getting closer to eternity all the time, on a twine chair—(Van Gogh) and me too—and it gets very depressing.

What can I do?

I had high hopes. We all did.

Remember just outside the Tangier Consulate:

"Have you met the Skipper yet?"

Later I did.

And now no skipping, no transport anywhere, except to a cut-rate mortuary.

Where were you when I wasn't there?

"Hound of Hell!!" screamed the Pop Star, and kicked the fink dog in the nuts.

"Only decent thing I done."

"Forget the whole thing. I have."

Great gasp at this point.

How much time? have I left?

Not much it seems.

January 30, 1997. Thursday

To Kansas City. Pleasant trip. Good breakfast at Nichols'. Back by the freeway.

David made an especially good dinner, small roast, thick, toothsome, and new potatoes and carrots and peas.

My god, how dull these English diaries can get.

I expect Trant—or is it Glen?—will soon be jolted out of his apathy—and his greenhouse, and his green iguana.

Fold sweet etcetera to bed with Ovaltine.

So what does happen?

"Trant thought the frescos were becoming more and more morbid—each of the Martyrs had died in a different way—one by roasting." (In a Rube Goldberg machine). "A saint carrying his own skin—lifelike in the extreme—the child was timing him to see how long he took" (to find out there was something to be tooked.)

He did something the others had not done: he laughed.

I once questioned in a dream an evil Italian Mountebank Spirit:

"Like, who are *you?*"

And he laughed and laughed—and went on laughing, in a marble dark lagoon, chintzy Italian decor—and he was deliciously evil.

As someone said about this evil spirit goes around sucking out the last breath from a dying youth:

"It was tasty."

The child looking quite radiant. He was in fact a Radiant Boy, suck the breath out of an old queen.

He's got a name, that Eyetye spirit—the Harlequin?

"You must leave now. Follow me."

Few things are less inspiring than muddy snow. It's an uncreative accident. (Bacon speaks of "the creative accident.")

A road of dirty, muddy snow splattered accidental enough—like a pig wallow.

January 31, 1997. Friday

Glen awoke rather late, for him, at 9:10 A.M., having held off till after 7:00 for his daily dose of G.O.M.

Most extraordinary coincidence—there is no such thing, but some things come close, like mud-splattered snow, or a hill of "snirt" in Dakota, where folks can quick-freeze and shatter like icicles when they go out for the mail.

"Snirt" is a thing of the spring.

If you make it through the cabin fever to the "snirt."

Winner take "snirt."

My overhead light suspended on a frayed cord, the whole socket is [an] inch from the ceiling, a line of white shows how long the canopy had kept dust and grime from its outline.

Reminds me of the "vile, dilapidated house of the evil old recluse" in Walter de le Mare's "Bad Company."

Now here is a recluse. What does he do with his time?

If he is an evil old recluse, he writes letters to *The Times* urging the "return of the lash." He amuses himself by hiring and firing butlers and cooks:

"Oh by the way, Williams, did you happen to see some change there on the mantelpiece?"

"No sir." (Dusting furniture.)

"Right there, where your hand is now."

"No, sir."

"Oh Williams, if you need an advance you can ask for it, you know."

Word gets around. If he isn't a recluse, he soon will be.

So the phrase "an evil old *recluse*" still bothers me. Can he be a black-magic man?

Oh it's drearier than that.

The lack of the overhead light lends a special dreary look to my bedroom, and the muddy snow outside and the gray-blue suburban landscapes. It's a Sudlow, for a dentist's waiting room. Streaks of dull russet ink.

Now a faint pink glow on the skyline, meaningless as child[ren's] art in kindergarten, progressive school.

Perlman writing—don't move your fingers—just your elbow—

William S. Burroughs
William S. Burroughs
Anne Oliver, Eugene
Angert, Dave Kammerer
this is elbow writing

And we got under tables draped with blankets, armed with stone axes. And I played Osiris in the school play, or one of them.

We used to compose the play and the [teacher] would write it down on the blackboard:

"I hear the tiger ate another baby last night."

"One doesn't feel safe with that tiger about."

(Looks about uneasily.)

I ask in this seedy hotel if she has a room.

"Yes."

She comes up from a basement staircase, and a big long-haired black dog comes up with her.

I never quite see the room—in this sleazy, sordid hotel.

The dog was friendly. He was black and shaggy.

People say I hate dogs. Not so.

People always like to pigeonhole one. Forty-five years ago I was "obviously on the verge of death from drink." Sixty years ago some English poet referred to me as "poor old Burroughs! Deep in addiction and hurting only himself."

How do *you* look at this point? Poor old Burroughs may look a shade better.

He is becoming, however, addicted to writing in these notebooks.

Still, what does an "evil old recluse" do, when he has shut himself [off] even from Covens and Covenants devoted to evil, where he will find suitable companions—perhaps even a soul mate—in spasms of pure evil.

Do not despair. You can still be eviler than Harlequin. He shrinks at your dank, cold, unspeakable vile emanations—plants wither and die under his presence.

But what I mean is: Evil needs Lebensraum. Room to live and breathe in.

How can any absolute hermit be evil?

He can give out a broadcast of such hate and evil as will take the joy out of every face, the bounce out of every stride, the gleam out of every eye.

"Towers Open Fire!"

On which side?

Doesn't matter. In the long run all sides are alike.

Don't get so long-winded!

He is eviler than any master black magician.

Why?

Because he *is*.

He didn't study, in a cellar, illuminated books of the Old Ones. No. He just stewed in the pure stuff. And it seeped into the walls, and the frayed, filthy carpets and drapes, and the whole vile house reeked of dirt, neglected and decaying.

He never had the comfort of rolling around in evil, like a dog rolls in carrion. Poor old cunt.

February 1, 1997. Saturday

Trant noted that the whole planet was moving in directions that he didn't like.

Take Lysol, for example. He liked the smell of carbolic. It was going to be replaced by the vile pine smell of a toilet in Grand Central.

And where was the Life Buoy carbolic soap? Gone. A friend brought him a cake of it from Iran. Lovely Boy Soap, it was labeled. Lovely Boy mysteriously disappeared.

And the old logo on Old Spice aftershave was an old [etching] of a four-master—now there is an abstract blob, a little boat with outsized sails. Gone all suggestion of spice, and opium and South Sea traders, Conrad. In its place a meaningless smear.

Little things. But they build up into a world I wouldn't want to make, or be a part of.

And the idiot War Against Drugs. And child molester hysteria. Like the leaders and their idiot constituents have taken leave of any senses they ever had.

Pick up any newspaper. Knock on any door. Fewer and fewer that one would want to see will answer your knock.

It's a slow, deadly takeover—by whom or what? Certainly inimical to me and anything I could represent.

Way they're digging up molested children in their dotage. Thirty years after. Next thing will be depositions from molested deathbeds.

Not just folly here. Sheer madness, desperately covering up. Bursting madness.

Call the plumber.

To describe the Dream City:

Area like a silent airport. I walk south. There is a square to my right. White. Open at top. Many doors. No one in sight, but menace is palpable. Radiating.

I can see now to the west, huge building, a thousand feet, some half-domes—I wonder what they look like from inside.

A corridor to an area of booths, tables, cages. I cannot see the top. I am attacked by small vicious dogs, but shoo them away.

At a semicircular table with chairs, like a lunch cart, is a beautiful youth, only three feet in height, made of some flexible ceramic, or alabaster, bright color. The youth does not appear to breathe, but he is alive in another sense that does not *need* breath. Or talk.

A door in front of me. I enter. Square room. White walls. About fifty feet to a side. Eighty feet [in] height. Like a surrealist picture—the one with bird houses.

Again, heavy feeling of danger.

Reading *Pan, God of Nature* by Leo Vinci.

Protagonist seeks the Great God Pan. He comes to the capo in a robe of deep red, trimmed with gold, that reaches the floor. (They sure go in for gracious living in the Kingdom.) Windows from cut sheets of flawless rubies, long canopy supported by seven ruby pillars.

The man says:

"Are you prepared to meet him?"

Many come under the primal law of the physical plane: duality. White or black. Good or evil.

That is—as Korzybski, founder of General Semantics, pointed out—"either/or thinking." Instead of "both/and"—

Basta—

When there is no longer any purpose or point in one's being here, one isn't.

Like the young man in Mary McCarthy's story:

"For no reason his heart simply stopped on the operating table."

Precisely: for "no reason."

The present trend on this planet is toward *control.* Make everybody a criminal, to make an *International Police State* necessary.

"War against drugs is a war against Dissent." (Drug Policy Letter)

Also a war against blacks—a third of young black males now in prison, on probation, awaiting trial, paroled (one slip and he slips back in)—

The whole scenario is blatantly obvious.

"We can't do it alone," wail the Malaysians, where hanging is mandatory for more than an ounce of morphine, eight ounces pot.

Citing Anslinger's tired lies:

"Why, he cut his mother's arm off when she wouldn't give him money for junk."

And so forth.

And now they are putting some Dutch queen in jail for sex with under-puberty boy—just a smudge of pubic hair—back in Amsterdam on the basis of depositions [by] the police in *Manila*. The fucking Philippines—and he draws four years.

"They will drive all the tourists away from us!" moan the boys of the world.

For the slum poverty of Manila, Morocco, Spain, Italy, a road out is now closed. A way out, like Bull Fighting, Soccer, Bicycle racing, is now closed. No more Prince Charming with Yankee dollars, British pounds—

"Too dangerous, old sport."

No more.

"Alone—no food."

Marlene Dietrich's diary—lying, of course.

The whole creaky structure is cracking, not quite wide open, it is just to the immediate advantage of so many quite decent people to keep it going.

After a lifetime of work some security, or just the means to fight for it.

Bastards trying to take our guns away from us. Looks like an alien invasion to me, boys, and their landing field is the human nervous system.

"We gotta go in there, 'Tunnel Rats,' and rat 'em out."

Anything that shows the two-thirds of [the spiritual] iceberg [that is] under water is anathema to the invaders. Emotion they will always try to degrade, or cheapen.

This is war.

Stand up and fight.

Fight what?

Start fighting, and you will soon find out who you are fighting. There is always a fight here. "This is a war universe."

My memory goes back to Majorca, where I spent a summer with my family, *circa* 1930. Goes back to knowing brother Mort has jacked off in the bathroom. No odor. I just knew.

"A faded summer love—

Beautiful to see,

but reminding me

of a faded summer love."

The bleak suburban landscape before me is a Sudlow. In every doctor's waiting room.

"Well, I've got some rather bad news. News from the bio-people."

"Well, is it?"

"I'm afraid it is."

As the old ones die, young ones garner the Brompton cocktails and other good things left behind. And I have nothing but good to say about it. Police corruption, drugs, why not? Loosen up, and it will be loosed unto you.

Simon? You see?

No, I don't see, but I want to see—
"and there are those who abhor light."
Well, maybe their eyes are too accustomed to darkness.
Nothing wrong with that.
Why can't I get back any of the Fears of childhood?
There still now.
No. Know.
So.

February 2, 1997. Sunday

Got a birthday coming up, sure as pricks and taxes. February 5, Wednesday. Can't say I welcome it.

Anderson, veteran Lawman, a dying breed of country sheriff. Why, in thirty-one years of law enforcement he never fired his gun, except to put down an injured animal.

We're all dying breeds, way I see it. World is going down into a very nasty police state. But the top people is caught in a bind— they have to [have] the criminals, vicious gangs, drug lords, drug war. A degree of chaos to justify an all-out war on dissent.

Before Communism died, that would have been the way for artists and intellectuals. Way closed. They subside into nothing. Don't need no street fighters. No brownshirts.

You want to destroy a species? Destroy its habitat, where it lives and breathes. What's left for the artist is a pile of "snirt." Identical houses to the sky.

No dissenting place? You have a dream maybe?

No dissent, no us, no drugs, no narcs, no crime, no flics.

So? Temporary measure stalling for time?

Time to do what exactly?

Certainly nothing to my advantage.

Nixon, late president, said Leary was "the most dangerous man in America."

Dangerous to who exactly.

How about a virus that *forces* the subject to speak the truth as he sees it.

You can't be too old.

February 3, 1997. Monday

Just found a fascinating book about Aliens, government cover-up. The Grays apparently [are] control Aliens, who have lost the ability to create, a dying race, that needs blood and semen from humans. Bad folk, those Grays.

I recall that Whitley Strieber was accused of working for the Grays.

Now this book has been here, I don't know how long, and I just read through it today.

Mighty loose ship, Burroughs.

Book answered a question in my mind:

Why are abductions and contacts always to mediocre or inferior minds? Why don't they come and see *ME*?

Because they don't want to, are afraid to contact anyone with advanced spiritual awareness.

The Grays want to make people stupider. Anyone with real perception is a danger to them. A deadly danger.

Once again I blame myself for lax and lazy and negligent behavior. I will send a note tomorrow. The book dates back to 1994—that is 3 years.

AIDS is spread by U.S. agencies who make deals with the Grays, to target "undesirables": niggers, spics and queers.

I can't believe they are quite *that* primitive. Niggers and spics, yes. Gays, no. Too many in high places. (Nixon used to refer to

J. Edgar Hoover as "that old cocksucker.") Any case, what sort of real dent in overpopulation is AIDS?

Horn mentions The Club of Rome as a big player in the global conspiracy game. They are heavy into cutting down population.

Me too, before they breed their peasant assholes into the sea.

He spoke at the Ecotechnics [Institute] meeting in south of France. Smooth.

"With full recognition of our mortality and all goodwill to all mankind."

Forget his name. Wouldn't you?

English or American, where they blend together.

I must catch up on all correspondence *mañana*—"the petty done, the undone vast."

I should have a system for processing incoming mail. My answers streak out like Mercury on jet-propelled skates of considerable complexity, shooting out a shower of sparks behind to burn holes in John Citizen's clothes. I turn and give him the finger, *and* a finger that shoots out—spurts out a cloud of sparks—

—remember old Fred Sparks. Looks like the whole *Time-Life* thing was working for the Grays all the time.

And what life was left?

So what can I do?

Hit them where they aren't, in the spiritual gut and a left hook with intuition, and a knee to the groin with plain country hate.

They got no feelings. And no solid waste.

As a reporter from *Life-Time-Fortune* advised me:

"Bitch Box 69. Check your balls here. If you want it, it's all urine."

This written out on a check from the United Bank and Trust Co., *Chemical* Bank and Trust Co.

A.J. rushes to the counter, laying bare his scrotum:

"Boy, check my bags."

"If you want it, it's all urine."
Clear enough from David Snell, reporter for *Time-Life*, with
Loomis Dean, photographer.

February 6, 1997. Thursday
Buckingham Palace is infested with beetles, mice and roaches.
Sue Lowe called—cancer—remitted by her meditations. She
lives at Truth [or] Consequences [N.M.]. Elephant Butte Lake.
[Across] Mesa.

February 7, 1997. Friday
How to describe Mary McCarthy's "Young Man," and "Walter
Ramsey" in Truman Capote's "Shut a Final Door"? Hopeless—
neither could ever receive grace.

All sorts of horrible people—torturers, secret police, the vilest
pimps and killers—could receive Grace—unlikely, of course.

Even politicians like Nixon, and Getty then? Truman? The
use of the Atom bomb when it was not by any stretch of expedi-
ency necessary, getting near to the unforgivable sin, since there
might not be anyone there to forgive it.

Stalin? Hitler? All the sorry lot of Dictators. More and more
unlikely candidates for Grace.

Always thinner, fading out into concentration camps, firestorms, cry havoc and unloose the dogs of war.

What red-blooded boy has not dreamed of "crying Havoc"?
The pure killing purpose.
I know.

Above: It's a basic *feel*—better than anything. It's the pure stuff,
burns you to searing white light.

All that tiresome old thing, now don't anybody try to get *physical* with me. I'm a Holy Man. Why even Sherifa, Jane Bowles's dream sister, said so.

I mean, I try at all times to be a Holy Man. A pure man.

And that's where we see how hopeless our [two] wretched way-below-anti-heroes are. How far from the possibility of grace—the concept—conception—of grace. They are the ultimate pariahs, for whom the most sensitive and perceptual reader cannot squeeze out a drop of sympathy, fellow feeling.

Are they hopelessly divided? That, of course.

In the Truman [Capote] story, the other is taking more and more tangible form. Sure, he could disconnect his phone—and *then*—

Why do these miserable assholes never engage my sympathy? Because they cannot admit that their viewpoint is inaccurate: "And I never will."

There is, at bottom line, a streak of pure iron in keeping an illusion of rightness. Almost religious.

Actually, one of the most evil creatures to crawl out of a latrine and look around for someone to be cruel to—yes, one of this tribe—said to me:

"I'll just travel around and be cruel to people."

I told him bluntly:

"You [aren't] near[ly] rich enough, and you could[n't] go up against any headwaiter."

True, of course. He *can't*, and desperately *wants* to, be cruel to people.

Let no short-sighted therapist loose this thing on the world.

Yes, imagine life under Absolute Emperor Walter—or the Young Man?

Shamefully, I would choose the Young Man—*although*, and of course *because*, I despise him even more than Walter. But

Walter is the more potentially dangerous of the two, and more unpredictable.

Now let us bring the two together.

My God, what a battle of super-heels.

So any sympathy to these subjects will, of course, simply strengthen their already unsightly constitution. Couldn't help them. Would simply be degraded by the Young Man into grating against Southern California, channeling, New Age.

Walter's complete lack of scruples turns up emotions which the Young Man immediately and expertly falsifies. Walter is at least capable of fear—the Young Man would mutter New Age platitudes.

And desolation—just turn the Young Man loose on that, with scraps of poetry, "Dover Beach"—a darkling plain—of *vernissages* and cocktails—

Where ignorant [bargains pass] by night.

His ravenous, lusty, fingers-down-blackboard, *agaçant* falseness eats all sincere emotion and shits out:

"The cancer patient at last!"

—as he draws in the screams which nourish him, to sing out lustily:

"Cast a cold eye on life"

(life withers under his fraudulent eye)

"Horseman, pass by."

Recall Cole Porter fell off a horse and his leg [got] infected and had to be cut off at the hip, and he went down from there, neglecting hygiene.

How a horse get into this?

Next morning he asks the nurse:

"I heard these terrible screams last night. Was that the cancer patient?"

"You'll never hear a sound from Mrs. Miller. Some patient in maternity, most likely."

"Ohh, oh—"

The lustiness drains out of him, like a ruptured condom.

"This is your pre-op medication."

Alcohol, and the wild eyes of Lotus Eaters—tired eyelids on tired eyes.

The surgeon said later:

"Only time I ever saw a perfectly healthy young heart simply stop, for no apparent reason, on the operating table."

No reason to keep going
on a darkling plain
a stranger and afraid
in a world he never made
told by an idiot
(I mean a sufferer from Down's syndrome)
Captain of his soul

Although seeking for a natural explanation, and always hoping for the supernatural, of course.

February 9, 1997. Sunday

Just typed the essay for Brad Morrow on "The Young Man" and "Shut a Final Door."

Fiction characters, will be a series—for example, "solid" characters like Councillor Mikulin, in *Under Western Eyes*. What a film that could make. And the French Naval officer in *Lord Jim;* unique characters like Jane Bowles and Denton Welch; fraudulent characters like the Major in *Adventure;* and the revolting Virginian.

Steve should [have] had a hide-out Derringer, and the other rustler a knife, and watch the Virginian go down.

All the Bar 20, John Wayne, Gary Cooper Law Men, the whole pestiferous lot of the Old West heroes and their villains—the same cardboard cut-outs, paper moons, muslin trees, false-front towns.

Young man hears these tasty screams, real toothsome screams, loud and throaty. And he sits bolt upright in bed with a hard-on.

"The cancer patient at last!"

Then he starts singing out lustily, and it gets—

Ibat res ad summa nauseum—the thing was becoming perfectly sickening.

Reference: Trimalchio's Feast, in memoirs of Petronius Arbiter.

I so admired him as a child—when he pulled out his dagger and killed a ruffian who was breathing wine into one's face—and Petronius just slid his dagger in, wiped it on the ruffian's toga as he fell, and walked on, as if nothing had happened.

February 10, 1997. Monday

In a sort of theater with someone. It was almost empty.

Who was with me, in a brown suit?

February 11, 1997. Tuesday

I was all of them: the cop, the informer, the thief.

Yes, that is what we writers sell: experience.

And painters? The Stendhal syndrome—*physical effects* [from] an art object.

Henry Geldzahler, in a lecture at Boulder, Colorado, said after seeing the work of Julian Schnabel [he was] not very much impressed. Then he promptly fell down the stairs.

Very good story: "To Feel Another's Woe," by Chet Williamson—twist on vampire theme.

How stupid so-called men fall all over themselves for it again and again. They disgust me!

As do all gutless American males. The woman gets all the gravy after living out three husbands, and still they scream for more.

The cranes and geese who mate for life and live to be 80 years old—repeat: 80 years old.

Friday, be my St. Valentine's massacre, [Santa] Meester William, *necesita*—

This is Saturday, February 15, 1997

The high discrepancy in price on the same item is awesome and pregnant with potential wealth. A sort of [usury] you understand. We publish competitive bids on the same item—the lowest being, of course, the winner—who is going to pay $49.95 for an item when next door he can buy it for $19.95.

The above situation of price fluctuation at unprecedented percentage exists only in the vast self-defense industry. "Unbeatable unarmed defense developed by Navy Seals under the Pharaohs of Ancient Egypt." Tear gases, stun guns, rubber bullets, bean-bag projectiles, blackjacks, sword canes, "every kind protection you need, Meester. Very bad peoples." We gotta keep those niggers on the job, and throw in some castrations, always hits a sucker where he lives. I mean below the belt.

I digress.

Who actually makes these items? A number of small [fly-by]-night loft and basement workshops.

Take my knife on a spring, cuts as you move through. Any profit possible? I doubt it.

We're getting back to 19th-century Daddy Warbucks idea. Garage, basement workshop—blossoms into starlets and swimming pools. But it is a wide-open field.

Take my sucker on the palms, the heavy overall compact of compressed air. Guaranteed to rupture eardrums.

You see, it's the most basic industry what there is: self-defense. Folk is becoming walking arsenals and the [slurs], far from killing them, is giving them strength and stamina, and a sustaining meanness.

Now our line is, we is ethical.

Ethical Self Defense—and all our relations.

While prices fluctuate, and quality suffers like a martyred saint, the Industry must falter and play into the waiting hands of the police and the military. Our Organization gotta [churn] the ethics angle—

Got no more punch than a constipated colonel.

Confucius say:

"Why try hold position already lost?"

Do they know how lost position is?

Look at suburban Lawrence, Kansas—trees, parts of houses, a road.

Where will this picture—a perfect Sudlow—be, three hundred years from now?

Look:

"The End. Terrible. I've seen it."

Lame Deer, a Lakota Shaman.

I was supposed to meet him, but we didn't make connections. Just look.

"Lived here? Did he? Who was he?"

"I can hear—"

Where human voices used to be, the empty vocal cords, the songs and symphonies, drums, flutes—all empty, just the chrysalis of sound shredding into dust forever.

Only the cats remain solid, demanding parts of myself.

I—what remains of I—

The cats are parts of myself. They owe their lives to me.
So what was it?
I don't—can't remember.
Something to do with a—
well, who knows anything at this point is not known.
So what was it?

We were told as boys to toast a marshmallow to a golden brown but never let it catch fire.

And here is the perfect Marshmallow Boy, tanned to a turn, with a fixed, sugary smile, face fixed in a congealing smile like cooling fudge.

The Marshmallow Boy who toasts the perfect 'mallow, never allowing his 'mallow to burst into flames—his face, a smooth mask, color of a seasoned meerschaum pipe (or a perfectly browned marshmallow), congeals into a smile like cooling fudge.

He holds aloft the marshmallow on a long three-pronged fork—eyes crinkled, heavy lids.

February 18, 1997

A ceramic boy with a full neck, white as alabaster, the lips precise, red, painted on. The neck long, searching. Bright red hair, violet eyes lit from behind. Growing up out of the floor.

He is hollow, like the boy at the bar in the sci-fi dreams of vast domes—under which are bars, ambiguous curtained baths and a bar this small (two feet high).

Porcelain boy, red hair, skin white as marble, he hardly moves, hardly breathes.

February 19, 1997. Wednesday

Dream—a boy with smooth marble face and red hair—beautiful and inhuman, like a ceramic. He seemed to be growing up from the floor—lips bright red and perfectly delineated—*painted* on flexible marble.

It was in a bathhouse of sorts.

I can capture no more, only the beautiful head, the long but full neck. His lower body seemed *emerging* from the floor, which is more and more, less and less, distinct. There is no floor, and he turns toward me. He is hollow.

This is, of course, the Ceramic boy in the sci-fi dream of huge domes and cupolas reaching up a thousand feet. The bar where I saw this porcelain boy, three feet tall. You could see he was alive— a faint breath.

February 20, 1997. Thursday

I was going to become a jewel thief. Some said:

"I envy you *your hands*. They look dead."

February 21, 1997. Friday

The plumber "Dirty Dave" arrived, finally, and fixed the toilet.

Reading *Asylum,* by [Patrick] McGrath:

"She brushed at a wasp that was buzzing around her glass."

Excellent detail to put reader *there*. Hard to ignore a wasp. No pun intended.

He's on the same wavelength as John le Carré. Quite skillful. (Talk about "damning with faint praise.")

Book is about this hot Madame Bovary affair between a mental patient and the wife of an important psychiatrist. (My spelling goes to Hell in a parachute.) Dreadful scandal. Lives blasted. A terrible thing.

But I am not in sympathy with Stella's adulterous lust.

Two careers languish inside me—a doctor:

"He was uneasy as a diagnostician."

Had a peephole, later TV. He would scan them all in the waiting room, and by the time they are ushered into his consulting room, he knew what was wrong.

He could be blunt:

"Mrs. Bently von Urschnitz, you have pancreatic cancer. I give you a month."

What I am writing here is lifeless and flat as old mud-splattered snow.

They have sucked my talent away. Why should I longer stay?

"It stinks and I am ready to depart."

George Sanders, I think.

"I leave you to this sweet cesspool."

Suicide note of George Sanders, actor, Barcelona. Overdose of sleeping pills.

"The sedge is withered from the lake
and no birds sing."

"How does it *feel* when your patch hatches?"

Skin patches of Fentanyl that hatch out at regular four-hour intervals.

February 22, 1997. Saturday

Last night I was going to become a jewel thief. Someone said:

"I envy your hands. They look dead."

Castaneda says to look at your *hands* in a dream. Mine were out in front, at elbow level. Plain old white brown hands. Nothing special.

A story about the hog town where they were feeding "dissidents and undesirables" to the pigs and exporting Virginia hams and pigskin jackets and boots and pants and vests.

When [they] started grinding up tourists and travel writers to feed the pigs, the shit finally hit the fan.

"Of course, we were looking for the won't-be-missed, but there were fuck-ups, involving a senator's daughter and so forth—all quite unfortunate."

Suggested by the story "Blanca," by Thomas Tessier.

Certainly cannibalism is the final answer to overpopulation and diminishing resources. Happened on Easter Island. The *indirect* cannibalism of the island of Circe, or Great Eastern or Ham Town or Swinesville.

The secret of the Virginia ham taste is to feed the pigs on peanuts for a fortnight before they are slaughtered, in the most humane and the least frightening manner, to avoid contamination from adrenaline.

("Meat from Brave Swine.")

And soon the prospective fodder was also fed on peanuts prior to being processed. Experiments will turn up exquisite dietary combinations that make the price of $100 a ham eagerly acceptable.

The climate is ideal, the prices low, so as to attract beatniks and layabouts, who form the essential wont-be-missed class. There are jobs in the processing plants, and workshops where pigskin clothes and gloves are produced.

The beatniks tend to be unreliable workers. A certain number of AWOLs from jobs, and they were hog feed. Drugs were easily obtainable, so the turnover was large enough to cover up.

Refugees were welcomed. (In many cases they did not get beyond the custom buildings, which were appropriately commodious to accommodate those in need of medical treatment and fattening up.)

Genetic scientists are working day and night to produce omnivorous cows and buffalo and deer.

This information is at the end of the story, sealed, the reader is asked not to open until he has read the account of some unfortunate travelers.

Then a questionnaire:

"Is there anything wrong with this laid-back place? If so, what and why? Have you glimpsed the Exchange Elite? Or the secret police intent on keeping secrets secret? Did anyone of your acquaintance disappear?"

Etcetera.

Now break the seal, and learn the truth.

Now you might think the disappearances would pile up. Like the beat chick who turns out to be a Senator's daughter—

There [he is], all red-faced and fat, screaming at *our* police, who reply with soft soothing:

"We think she may have changed her name and moved to . . . We will know more in a few hours. And now I *suggest* that you return to the Long Pig Hotel and *rest.*"

His hand on the Senator's arm is firm and official.

"So the Senator suffered a heart attack in *our* hotel, death certificate by *our* doctor."

She should yield some tasty chops, and the hermetic beauty of it: even her bones has been ground up and fed back to the pigs.

I say always stick with what we have. No need to be expanding Swinesville to cover the planet with hams.

Any case, the feud that sprung up like a deprived prick between the Cow Peoples—the Ruminators—and the Wild Boars was a spectacular. When the smoke clears you know there is, of course, a Romeo-and-Juliet routine:

"Swine, swine—wherefore are thou swine?"

He is from the original Swine Elite, and she is from the old Ungulates.

Always looking for trouble:

"Smells kinda like pig garbage in here, Clem."

"Well now maybe it's bull shit you're smelling, from your own ass."

"Everybody hit the deck!"

Somehow it don't ring true—it's flimsy and don't come alive. It's got no Stendhal.

February 23–24, 1997. Sunday, Monday

And I hear someone say:

"I envy your hands. They look dead."

And Bitch Box 69:

"Hey, boy, check my bags," says A.J., baring his scrotum.

"If you want it, it's all urine."

(From [David] Snell of *Time-Life-Fortune*, to me in 1959.)

One more thing to learn, and always too late.

They have no stomachs, and in consequence *no solid waste. It's all urine.*

I guess they have given up on me.

Any case, we shall see.

If we have to, we will.

February 25, 1997. Tuesday

It was in 1948 or thereabouts, with Kells Elvins. We were raising cotton in Pharr, Texas, and came across this story in *Time* about Harlan County in Virginia.

This cop described as a "buck-toothed, snarling gunman, who took his pleasure from pistol-whipping bootleggers and cussing out their women folk."

Now that sort of pleasure can be unhealthy.

One Saturday evening the square is full of folks, in town for the week's shopping, and this cop walked over to question four characters in a parked car—

"Something not right about them folks."

Well, shots erupted, and the cop snarled up blood and dropted to the pavement.

I was a Boy Scout at the time, so I turned him over on his back to assess the extension of his injures. It was my plain first-aid duty.

Now, plain salt is one of the best antiseptics that can be got, and I had a box of it I'd just boughted. Morton salt—"When it rains it pours." So I poured. I sprinkled half the box on his perforations. Four—I counted, each one the size of a quarter. Now salt on perforations like that can smart a man, but he was past smartin'.

I look up and the square is empty, just sun on old red brick, and his long yaller teeth *a-shining in the sun.* Nobody saw anything or knowed anything. Just as well.

There was FBI Feds from Washington nosing around, like he'd been "deprived of his civil rights," but nobody had sawed anything, and nobody knowed nothing.

Well, rights for the wind and good riddance to a "buck-toothed snarling gunman."

Bits and flotsam of my past—all dreary, inept, always way below my level.

At 83 just emerging from a stormy adolescence, costly to myself and those around me. Of course, no more nonsense "love" at my old age.

Ruski was my last love. My first

cat.

He showed me what Love is. The love of a species.

Millions of bright-eyed kittens, weasels, cats—

"I made these animals."

"Centipedes, scorpions, spiders? Why? Why?"

"As a final threat!"

The Centipede Troughs—the man tied to a couch while a foul centipede arches over him.

Now remember, they didn't have horror stories in those days. Nor sci-fi.

So where could an idea like that emerge from?

March 1, 1997. Saturday

"I'd give *anything* to have my talent back. Then all I'd need would be a room and a typewriter—and—"

"No glot. Clom Fliday."

Now, "I'd give anything" are the words that summon the Devil, or an accredited agent with a bargain. But they deal only in quantitative merchandise, like Time. Money. Junk.

So I want to buy talent, qualities, skills—even some wise guys want to be a Saint.

"Take your business to weeping Jesus for chrissakes. We don't handle that kinda goods."

I want to write something will really knock them outa their socks.

Ever see that? Car wreck knocked the man right out of his shoes. Shoes and blood and gasoline all over Canal St. A truck lost its breaks—I mean *brakes*—and smashed into cars at a stop light. I was living at 210 Centre St. Brion came in and told me about the pileup on Canal.

We were working on *The Third Mind* at the time. Cut-ups— how the word can translate into solid event, accident.

Event
Accident
make a dent?
Let's invent
News events
and
accidents.

Now that Dream Machine Vampire had a funny kinda smell about him, like unknown offal decaying in alien alleys—

Reeking urine of the Grays. Phosphorescent excrement of the Blues—[on] a long intergalactic trip they sometimes retain it for months—excrement of the Blues, who live on minerals and phosphorus. It glows in the dark and conveys a deadly form of radiation sickness, should an unfortunate pilgrim step in it.

(Corny.)

Incredible slums of disease and famine, crawling beggars hold out stumps of rotten arms, with great white worms protruding and writhing, in mendicant postures. (Some of the worms have tiny hats.) The smell of these vile slums can double you over like a kick in the balls.

And they sleep in their own filth, prize it and use it for mortar in their insect warrens and the corral area.

I recall at Harvard that old cunt Professor talking about Mecca, and the "unspeakable depravity of the Arabics."

"Gentlemen, *unspeakable!*"

He leans forward onto the podium, enforcing a reverent silence, charged with pure *hate.* The way only an evil old religious woman can [distill] it, over and over, down over the years.

(Those withered old cunts could learn something from the Professor: "Things you didn't know existed.")

The old fuck pulls his parts together. His power is coming. He points to a cringing youth:

"I will ask that gentleman, who slept through my lecture, to step up here, please."

He was a huge man. Six foot four, 250 pounds. He charges at the boy:

"Your name?"

(Etc. I left at this point.)

"I'm sorry, sir."

"You are indeed, and you should be. I am passing your case along to the Holy Man."

The boy faints. He knows what that means in Egypt: capital cases are passed along to the Holy Man, who *always* confirms the sentence. (It would rock the country to its pyramids if he didn't.)

So your case passed to the Holy Man was a death sentence.

At the insect slums. Looking for action, not too far-out, the bar in a stinking alley.

He looked around the cubicles, there was something stirring in his groin. He threw back filthy reeking bedclothes. His cock was throbbing, as it sprouted the hairs, pincers and claws of a centipede. The smell of this vile—

No words can do it, I can't.

So what could smell like that? What could be the *source* of such a smell?

A smell he had never before smelled—vile, putrid—

Words sink into wasted grids—words plastered over with words.

Drugs in these slums? A burnt-out insect hulk in six months.

And for those who can pay: immortality drugs. Can drag a man or a woman out, over forty years maybe, by playing it a little bit at a time—like the Galápagos tortoises, who live five hundred years maybe . . . *real slow.*

So what is the point of life? Conflict, of course. No conflict, no life.

The Grays have *run out of conflict.* They all get to be the same.

(A huge loft stretching out of sight in a gray haze. Now and then everybody leaps up and attacks his neighbor. Then slump back into their stupor.)

Back to the slums, the nitrous rotting film, garbage—

Old actors never die, they just fade away on old screens.

So I am not writing it.

Start with a Hero.

He has been through the secret school, junk habit, withdrawal, the lot. He works for no government or political group.

Already hopelessly corrupted by the Grays?

By corruption itself. The temptation of power. The corruption of power.

So who wants to keep us *here* on this wretched planet they have devastated?

Those who desperately *need humans.*

Of course, for reproduction—but there is more: for *Energy.* [That's] why this is a fractured planet: THEY need our Energy. They must keep the planet divided.

There was no friction. Everybody agreed with everybody because everybody was everybody—all cloned.

It all rained down.

It all rained down.

Orgone balked at the gate.

Christ bled.

Time ran out.

Thermodynamics has won at a crawl.

"We'll build viler slums!"

Make the Moral Majority spit up their rotten guts with rage.

We gotta new "A.S."—Anger Serum. It hits the Bible Belters, *and* it hits them [and] hates them 100%:

"*Le Rage!*"

Demented people—naked, with erections, armed with rusty pipes, pitchforks, hammers, butcher knives—prowl empty streets.

Don't do nothing to anybody else, you be scared of having it done to you.

Scared, or disinclined.

This don't hold more water than a sieve.

[An S&M] beats a solid commuter, and the commuter beats him back, and he fucking loves it.

It don't work. It doesn't hold enough water to wash your teeth in. Abort it, STAT.

Caught in NY beneath the Ides of the Stomach. The Piper in Uncle Sam drag, pulled down the paper sky—the great big boofull sky.

Loud and clear—through London—through London—emerging—widespread [petting] in chow lines—as a personal thing—

"My whippets are dying."

"You might be a man about it."

Pig place. It was incredibly green and fertile, with *bone* meal.

March 3, 1997. Monday

Bright sunny day. With a chill on it.

"We'll meet again."

James drove me to K.C. because we didn't go on—don't know when—Thursday as customary.

Nichols' closed. Don't know why. We eat at Waid's. Poor-dressed, limping, ugly patrons. Nice waitress. Just call, and she will hear you.

"I know we'll meet again some sunny day."

Bright sunny day.

We'll meet again.

James droved me
    to K.C.

Because we didn't go on—

Don't know where—

Thursday

As customary

Don't know when

Nichols'

Closed—

Eat at Waid's

Nice waitress—

"If you want an Angel near you,

Just call and she will hear you."

Good food.

I deplore runny fried eggs. These were firm, the yolks sticking up like teen tits.

"I know we'll meet again,

some sunny day."

"The blind fools!"

This is the Domesday thing—

End of "life" as it

was called, on Planet Earth
Planet Earth, as it was called.
"We'll meet again
Some sunny day."
"I know we'll meet again
Don't know where? When?"
Voice fading out "some sunny day"
Light fading.
"We'll meet again—"
(voice weakens) "some
sunny day"—always weaker.
"I know we'll meet again.
Don't know where? Don't know
when"—voice fading out—
sun fading, day fading.
A blast of light—action—camera.
"Some sunny day."
A trillion light bulbs blow out and darkness falls forever where no light can be.
(That's a bit bombastic.)
A vista of sun on water, red brick, marble, paintings, animals, trees and forests, mountains and deserts, a vast panorama of what Homo Sap has done.

A visit with Carl Laszlo to a Swiss Baron. He had a gun room, a Nogant Gas-seal Russian pistol. The hall was lined with the horns of chamois.
"You killed them all?"
"Of course, or they would not be there."
"Obviously."
He shot me a clouded look.

Later, over some heavy cake with coffee at 3 P.M., the Baron said, apropos of what I forget:

"I like to shoot cats."

Too bad I met him too early, or I would have made myself clear:

"Devoted cat lover myself."

I stand up and kick his dog (rather small) in the ribs.

The Baron stands up, outraged—dog yelps and goes to ground.

"I am at your disposal," I say graciously.

By now we are both in 18th-century costumes—

enough—

I kill him, of course, with a ball in the neck.

1. Ruski.
2. Virginian
3. Snarling gun man.
4. They do not always remember.
5. The Priest they called him
6. Dying feeling—Dr. Dent: "What the American narcotics dept. is doing is *evil*," of course it is.
7. Changes in Brion's room 32 at 9 rue Git-le-Coeur.
[8.] Bar of the Chelsea, NYC. Filliou of the Domaine Poetique beside me at the bar. He says: "How many times did they try to *kill* you?" Protecting my "plot" has been a Pyrrhic victory. Winner take nothing.
[9.] "The Young Man," and Truman Capote ghost stories. Most difficult of all mediums, except sci-fi. I must write one with the real chill up the back of the neck.

I hope I can write *something* before I buy the farm.
Something with the heavy Stendhal Syndrome.

Like I felt about the dream in *The Heart Is a Lonely Hunter:* carrying this basket, terrible bright sun, no one sees him, and the horror of carrying this basket and not knowing where to put it down mounts, until he wakes up groaning.

I read this passage and I got the chill up my neck, when I asked myself the question:

"What is in the basket? What is in the basket?"

Terrible bright sun, famine in all the Near East[ern] faces, all walking. No one talking, walking under the terrible sun, and he had a basket he had to put down somewhere. He carried this basket for a long time. Where can he put it down?

So my obituary is written.

Why shouldn't I contribute?

"He was generous of himself. Anybody who asked got from him. He had to give. It was all he had."

March 4, 1997. Tuesday

Meet with the heart doctor tomorrow at 12:45.

March 5, 1997. Thursday—today is Wednesday— writing Wednesday

Egg blue sky outside.

March 7, 1997. Friday

A sex affair with somebody I never saw before. Rather stocky, dressed in blue. We are separating on bad terms. He says:

"I don't know whether I can do that kinda love in my haunches."

Same character, bitter hate between us.

Who could this be?

He is rather short and stocky, always dressed in a blue shirt??

March 8, 1997

Reading *The Last Don*—page 36.

Lady has a stalking husband name of Boz. Dangerous. Always escalates, throws water in her face at the Pavilion.

It will be the *real* thing next.

Only one solution to the Boz problem: total.

And to many others, like the creep who said:

"Burroughs is an old bitch," slopping out flat beer.

Well, Pal, would you like to come here and expedite matters? (It's pistols at ten paces.)

I doubt it.

Only a coward, a whiner, a loser would come on like that.

I would be happy to accommodate.

And the one who said:

"The fact that you exist is an insult to me."

"So there ain't room for both of us in this universe? Fill your hand, Pilgrim."

He got no hand to fill, being just a voice on the answer machine. Familiar voice of the argumentative, semieducated, ambivalent. (I bet he has red hair and beard. I can *see* him now. He wants to talk. He always made his way by talking.) Calls me a "literary poser."

In another message:

"I thought you might like to know that Kerouac is in town. Back from the grave. With a good Catholic prick. I thought Bill would like to know this."

"Where are you? On tour? I *need* to know."

Last message six years ago.

Now the more the exposure, the more the danger.

(I carry a .38 snubbie on my premises, at my belt at all times. I leave the door open. Someone walks in with something in mind, he won't walk away.)

Recall who was on the front cover of *Time,* and looking quite unwell too, but Verwoerd, and a short time later a congressional messenger lunged across his desk with a Fairbain knife, and did him right in.

Said he had a demon tapeworm in his gut. When he walked by some good food the worm would get the scent and glug out: "Gimme some of that!"

Mr. Verwoerd, him dead.

Well, legalized dueling would liven things up, and keep some civil tongues in stupid mouths.

I will pay for a one-way ticket here. And any funeral expenditures that you may incur or occur or accrete. With a tasteful stone angel springing from your decomposition. *And* a bell in your *hand,* in case burial was premature.

There will be, of course, competent physicians and ambulances to meet the emergencies which will, of necessity, arise.

So who is this handsome unknown?

A composite perhaps, but something new has been added.

In this era of overpopulation, the old kill-a-million-niggers, press a button and kill ten thousand—a million chinks, or niggers, or gooks is no longer applicable.

Look at cloning. I see loft and basement "cloning camp," as they are called. No stopping it. When they can, they will, and they can now.

I could relate to being cloned.

"Why not?"

Last words of Timothy Leary. I talked to him shortly before he shuffled off these mortal coils.

Why not?

Why not?

Timothy Leary's last words to me were:

"Why not?"

What gives a clone?

About who clones who, or why, or when.

So the world ends with a sigh.

What a predictable bore.

March 9, 1997. Sunday

They even went out to interrogate old man Ellisor. He is sitting there on his porch, with a mason jar of Georgia White by his hand.

Two of 'em. One comes on all folksy—fake folksy—phony folksy:

"How about givin me a snort of your bug juice?"

Arch hands the jar over slow and steady, not spilling a drop.

"Be my jest."

(Arch does a lot of reading into deep things like that.)

And the other Fed is waving the Witness Protection Act in front of old Arch, his pale, faded-out blue eyes, with cataracts that moved around like silver clouds crossing a noon sun.

"Going to be a sizzler."

And they both stand there with hands on their hips, a mite paunchy from three-martini lunches, and look at him reproachfully.

"We gotta job to do."

"Well, get to doing it."

"You don't have to live in a shack like this. You could have an apartment with TV and refrigerator and flushing toilet. And $50 a month, clear and free. It's the chance extraordinary!"

"Got what I need right here. My grandpappy's grandpappy came out here like two hundred years ago, and wasn't nothing in this patch of pine hills but owls. Hoots and Ellisors. Been here sixty years, don't aim to move."

The Feds look at each other and shrug. No use fucking with this old fart.

This bodyguard top man. His arm moves itself with flashing speed and—"you and me we shoot perfect sometimes." His arm always shot perfect. The Always Arm. He is looking at the target. His arm does the rest.

Ultimate horror story: The centipede prick.

I repeat, with no friction, no conflict, any system will run down—some quicker than others, but they all keep the home fires burning, though the hearts are yearning. . . .

"It's a long way to Piccadilly, it's a long way to go."

"Comin' in on a wing and a prayer."

"Though there's one motor gone, we can still carry on,

"Coming in on a wing and a prayer."

Utopia. Where is the challenge? Where is the fear? Where is the enemy?

This is a war/fear planet, predicated on war and fear—

Face Fear—from all over, it's falling into pieces.

"Well, what are we waiting for? Washington, D.C., is right down that road."

Kicking in liquor stores, loading up at the hardware, taking on .22s, 12-gauge shotguns, any weapon at hand. Reeling drunk already.

March 10, 1997. Monday

Remember that island off Venice. Alan and I. Waiting for a boat back to Venice.

We are sitting at a table in front of café, a square, everything in worn limestone. And a young man in the middle of the square. He was moving, dancing, waving his arms to some music he could hear there in the square.

This was a frequent performance, very Italian, very difficult to describe or convey. The music is totally unknown to me and totally hostile. I have rarely felt more heavily attacked and defeated.

Always occasions when I have been totally humiliated: the dry cleaner in Tangier by the Turkish bath; the café in Paris; the butcher meat store in New York recommended by Wilson (who had been a foreign service operative in South Africa); the stationery newsstand in London:

"Merry Christmas."

"Be nice to me."

Abject defeat.

The stirring [—], like heat waves around the target, spiraling in (often on a cold sore), gray filaments settling in, marking for death. Cold sore on his face, cringing fear.

The performance on that nameless island—I cannot even indicate. It was expressing the whole island's rejection of me, so complete that they were unaware of it, leaving this twitching puppet to enforce its will.

"Bill, kill!"

It was a very rarefied form of pantomime he was doing, a very old and special act.

"God damn you gone crazy.

God damn you fucking lazy."

His act involved other actors, it is all so hazy. I am drinking ouzo while I wait for the boat.

What boat?

Ouzo brings scant relief from . . .

Last chapter on the gunman:

So the Feds sent people down there. The buck-toothed snarler has been deprived of his physical rights, being dead like that. But nobody had sawed nothing.

Two of them even droved out to see Old Arch Ellisor.

"Howdy. We work for that *crazy* American government."

Old Arch is sitting there on his porch with a mason jar of white corn by his hand.

Then one fed, both had suits and ties and black shined shoes, comes on fake-folksy:

"How about giving me a snort of your bug juice, Pardner?"

Arch passes him the jar.

He takes a swig and says, "Phew!" and goes into an act, fanning himself.

And the other one is waving the Witness Protection [Act] in Arch's face:

"You don't have to live in a shack like this. You could have a nice place in town—TV, flushing toilet, $50 a month clear and free and all yours. It's the chance extraordinary."

They stand, hands on hips, and look at him heavy.

"We got a job to do."

"Well, get on with doing it some place else."

That was it. They went back to Washington or wherever they comed out of.

Who is this unknown lover of my dreams.
 I hate him always for his neglect of me.
 Why? Who?
 Do I care?
 But I do.

March 11, 1997. Tuesday (subject to correction)

Usual good news about women drowning their children, dousing a roommate with gasoline and setting her on fire.

Man bites the prick off an 83-year-old man in drug rehab clinic. Woman drowns her two children in a bathtub. [Woman] douses her roommate with lighter fluid and sets her on fire (she dies):

"She wouldn't get up."

Man killed another motorist at stop sign:

"He was driving too slow."

Ho hum.

Whole planet in a hopeless checkmate. They have to have friction—war, fear, death—to keep the machine from running down.

All utopias are bullshit. Without challenges the human scroll runs down like an old record.

"How dull it is to pause, to make a rest . . . not to shine in use."

Sounding the battle cry of freedom—

"and he conquered all the Injuns come within his sight."

("The Battle Hymn of the Republic" has fallen from my mind.)

"He has sounded forth the bugle that shall never call retreat."

"Allons, enfants de la patrie"—

always fainter more distant—

"In the land of the free and the home of the brave"—

darkness and silence.

Chaos in Africa. The Hutu hacking up the Tutsi.

Pestilence—Ebola, famine, war and death.

Peace to all men?

Recall this old movie, the Cossacks and the Mongols. The Czar sends an ambassador to say the fighting has to stop. (I think John Gilbert acted in it. Forget name of the film.)

The head man says:

"Stop fighting the Mongols? We have nothing else to do. Sit here until our bellies roll over our knees?"

"Those are the words of the Little Father."

Final resumé:

"The men must fight,
the women must work,
and over all is God."

Good a way as any, out of the basic impasse: blind alley. Dead End.

No friction, no energy. No energy, no life. No enemy, no friction. No enemy, no life.

War, Plague, Famine, Death.

All orchestrated by the vicious macho male.

So now Peace descends. All males are castrated at birth. No more fights. No more trouble. Everybody moves slower and slower. And finally not at all. Run down like an old wind-up clock.

Nick Smart. March 18. Wants to cross-check my relation with him.

I am a Commander of [the Order of] Arts and Letters, conveyed by Jacques Lang, Cultural Minister of France.

March 12, 1997. Wednesday

Why I woke up? Some mosquito enemy woked me up.

Have I ever got a hot film property:

The extraterrestrial Grays are a dying race. They cannot reproduce. There is no friction, no conflict in their culture. They have solved all their problems, all too well. Little Gray men.

What now?

Cherchez la femme, what? *hein?*

So the young human falls heavy for a glamorous Gray. They have an offspring.

Enter the power of hate and bigotry and evil. Tragic scenes of course, but in the end a wise old Gray confronting the Priest who has stirred up the mob, says:

"We too have made mistakes—too monstrous for remorse to tamper or to dally with. There may be something left of our fading race, something of value. We can only hope."

I can hear the dreadful dialogue:

"So," he snarls, "to you I was just some sperm in a test tube to prolong your vile vampiric life."

"No, John, there was more—I swear there were moments when I felt the human feelings of love and beauty, grief, and the terrible sadness. This we have shared. You cannot deny that moment, that incandescent millisecond when we were one."

John throws himself on his Gray. Her abdomen is already pulsing with life. John helps her to a sofa. Not a moment too soon. She bursts in a great cry of pain and ecstasy. The child emerges.

(My Muse fails me at this point.)

The purity and sadness of a dying race. There were so many solutions. Class structure based, of course, on physical differences. Well, the fact that it did not *work* shows the closing options.

"Perhaps from our failure something of value can be salvaged. We can only hope."

(Hope music.)

No one believes it—but who is no one?

March 12?, 1997. Wednesday

On a train in a compartment. Green covers.

Well, if we arrive alive—

The train is going downgrade doing 90 mph. We are due to arrive at 6 P.M.

Someone opens a ledger book, like:

"Yes, 6 P.M."

March 13, 1997. Thursday

On a train going very fast (90 mph). Green upholstery. I wonder if we will get there—St. Louis?—alive. We are due in St. Louis at 6 P.M.

March 13, 1997. Thursday

Just got idea for the Alien film script:

We start with a montage of war scenes, all times and places. It all fades out. The Alien slumps in the horrible depression of stasis.

Wise old Alien:

"You can't get away from the old law: Conflict = energy = life = friction = energy = life. No conflict, no energy, no life. This is a war Universe."

Peace, Utopia, Paradise?

No energy = no friction.

Next is a party. There are little scenes in curtained alcoves, where the fate of nations is balanced and decided. We need to suggest the most high-level and informed actors, with access to supersensitive information, including the relations of high government officials with Aliens—the Grays, who can assume any guise, feign any emotion, seemingly without feeling—cold, glamorous beings.

However they are in fact extremely insecure, to the point of terror. They cannot reproduce, they are experimenting with human hybrids.

The essential impasse. Conflict creates energy. No conflict, no energy. They desperately need our energy, so they are dedicated to fomenting disorder, conflict and war.

Some of them see this deadly blind alley. The hard-liners do not.

On Earth the chaos and conflict [have] become a deadly threat to all players. To impose total order would deplete energy levels to a dangerous point.

People just can't get out of bed, go to work, shave, bathe. People with their shirts hanging out of their pants, shaving with battery razors on the subway, sleeping past their stop.

Whole machine is winding down.

Over and out.

March 14, 1997. It was a Friday

"The Ides of March have come."

"Aye, Caesar, but not gone."

"Upon what meat does Caesar feed that he has grown so fat?"

Forget it.

Two of them droved out to see old Arch Ellisor, out where the sheep dip used to be and Clem Higgins got drunker than usual, fell into the dip, got stuck and drownded. Some said his four-teen-year-old daughter he'd been screwing incestuous held him down by jumping on top of him, up and down like they was screwing—and some says it was his old lady dumped a bag of hog feed on him, you know them dips is constructed like what a bitch has between her gams.

So here they stand, in suit and tie and black shined shoes, like they sprung up outa some place real different.

And there is Old Arch sitting on his porch, a mason jar of white corn by his hand.

And they say it together:

"We work for that *crazy* American government."

And Arch says:

"Howdy."

Then they split up. One comes on fake-folksy:

"Hey, Pilgrim, how about giving me a snort of your bug juice?"

Arch passes him the jar.

He takes a swig:

"Phew!"

Goes into an act of fanning his mouth.

The other Fed is waving the Witness Protecting Action in Arch's face:

"You don't have to live in a shack like this. Why, you can have a nice place in town, TV, flushing toilet *and* $50 a month, clear, free and all yours. How's that hit you?"

And he leans forward, punches Arch—soft and playful—on his chin.

Then they both gets hands on their hips, and their eyebrows shoot up and wriggle:

"It's the offer you can't refuse."

"It's the chance extraordinary."

And they is back smiling—"we know you"—a knowing smile:

("He's hooked, we got him. He is ours.")

—as they smack their lips.

"We got a job to do, Arch."

"Same as you."

"Just what sorta work you do, Arch?"

"Well now, I sorta steer folks the way they wanta go. Like someone comes here wants some action, comes to Old Arch."

Suddenly they stop the smiles, and chew up the words and spit 'em out.

"You was there."

"You saw it."

"Ever hear about obstructing justice?"

"We can summon you to Federal Court, and when you lie it's a felony."

They prance around him, jabbing fingers at him.

"Want to go into the can, Arch? Old ones like you do hard time."

Arch brings out his fiddle.

As they caper around and 'round, faster—faster—

Never found hide nor trace of those two FBIs.

"Hi diddle diddle, the cat and the fiddle, and the cow jumped over the moon."

Arch is shedding his old-man suit and dances out in the goat skin as Boujeloud of the Bacchanal, with his flare—a touch will make any gash pregnant within the year.

Reminds me of a great Arab story I heard. Difficult to recreate without gestures:

His wife is pregnant. They are in the marketplace. An unknown approaches like a beggar, leers at her swollen belly, and strokes the harelip on his own evil and ugly face.

Too late, the husband intervenes:

"*Que hace, hombre?*"

He shoves the man away, the man sniggers, strokes his harelip and fades into the market.

Needless to say, the child is born with a harelip.

The vague watery blues of an old man's eyes looking back to Romany Marie's, and once I won a double—about $103.

The bookie paid me with no smile.

March 15, 1997. Saturday. My day

Remember buck-toothed Eleanor Roosevelt and her "MY DAY."

As Hemingway said:

"She had great charm."

What is charm? Something sincere, outgoing, and pleasant to see.

Some folks get sincere, and something unsightly emerges.

Back to old Wizard Arch Ellisor with—two Feds prancing around him, jabbing their fingers at him.

"Know what they done in Marion Pen?"

They thrust their snarling faces at him.

"They fucked a ninety-five-year-old paralyzed man up his ass."

"He had a rectal hemorrhage."

Arch says:

"I reckon."

"I wouldn't want to see that happen to *you*, Arch."

He shoves his face an inch [from] Arch's, leering, all his teeth out.

They are going manic. They grab the jar of corn and swig.

Suddenly, from nowhere, Arch manifests a fiddle. His face is shifting, animals peeking in and out—goats and cats and weasels. He is dancing, cats gather and yeowl.

"Round and round, faster and faster."

The Feds is capering, leering.

"Take off your coat and throw it in a corner."

The Feds take off their coats, showing their shoulder holster guns (which they pat and rub suggestively), drop their coats over the porch rail.

"Stay all night and stay a little longer,

Don't see why you don't stay a little longer."

On the way back to town a "freak wind" blew the Fed car off the road. Both agents were "killed at the scene."

"It was a terrible tragedy," said Bill Rogers, spokesman for the FBI office in Pitsman, [Montana]. "They were brilliant young operatives, with a grasp on sensitive cases. It is a tragic loss to the department, and the nation."

March 16, 1997. Sunday

Reading *The Last Don,* interesting work.

It seems a hit man is not allowed to enjoy his work. They say that he has a "bloody mouth," and decent Mafiosi don't like it.

"Dante," accused of a bloody mouth:

"I'll enjoy my work less, if that is what you want."

Bad form, old boy, not to like it as a job well done—but when it comes to rutting around in it like a dog rolls in carrion, The Family draws a strict line. It is unsightly to snarl and let your hair stand up and the glow go on behind your eyes and the rutting smell reek out of you.

Now "Pippi" is out on a job with him, and he says it was downright *disgusting,* and the stink steamed offen him was a turn-on [of] its own.

You said:

"*What* could give out a stench like that?"

He is breathing heavy, in and out through his teeth, and his *eyes* is *eating*—disgust you to see it.

The Don reached a conclusion: he will write the horror books, and make the horror films.

Remember:

"The sedge is withered from the lake, and no birds sing."

Pornography is a potent weapon, directed through penny arcades, movies, sleazies.

It's all winding down.

No place—

Remember how my grandfather, who invented the Burroughs Adding Machine, was so discouraged with his models that he hurled them from his window into a vacant lot.

The next morning he had the answer, as simple as a cylinder full of oil with apertures, will guarantee same figure no matter how the lever is pulled.

Bravo, Granddad—who died of consumption in the Piney Woods.

You can go and see a stained-glass memorial:

"Sacred to the memory of William S. Burroughs."

It was a long time ago but not too far to walk, just right here where the old sheep dip used to be till the time Old Man Higgins fell in the dip and got stucked and drowned. Some folks say his fourteen-year-old daughter he was screwing jumped on top of him and rode him down into the dip. It comes down, see, like a V—like a V for vagina—and Arch Ellisor had a quitclaim deed to the property. Moved in, that was back in the Forties, I reckon.

They even took on Old Wizard Ellisor, and droved out to see him.

"Stay all night and stay a little longer.

Take off your coats and throw 'em in a corner."

Driving back to town, the car containing the two Feds was strickened by a freak wind, droved it off the road, and the two agents were killed and pronounced deadly at the scene. It was a terrible tragedy.

Remember the Canadian bank robber, circa 1916. He had the sweetest voice any bank teller or witness ever heard:

"Everybody, please. Put your hands up high."

One was advised to believe it. He said that when he killed someone, he got a "terrible gloating feeling."

I think he was killed in a shoot-out with police, if my memory serves.

It was a long time ago.

March 17, 1997. Monday

Garbage put-out day.

Mutie is ill. The lady vet came to get her yesterday. When she wouldn't eat, I knew she was sick.

Call today. Yes, high white [blood cell] count, couldn't eat all day Sunday. Ate and threw up Monday morning.

Most startling discovery: a *pellet* in her body. Not recent, since there is no apparent entry wound. .22? Air gun? I don't know if surgery is indicated.

Like to get my blackjack on that son of a bitch.

Like what my Wasp relations, the two Lee sons . . . when my name is mentioned, they say:

"*That* son of a bitch."

Contrast how the Don treats his retainers: at least a slot machine concession in Mound City, Illinois.

For me—from the "public relations" family that came up with the name of "Press Releases," the shiny new dimes the old withered man would pass out (some smart kid should have tossed back: "Well I figure you need it more than I do.")—bastards.

From them for me, absolute "Zilch."

And me, ready to hit the head competitors.

The Wasps make all these laws against drugs and booze and gambling, and who creams off the gravy? Decent American bastards like me and the kid next door. Never the fucking wops, and spics, and chinks, and blacks.

And we get kicked around like Pariah dogs:

"Don't want your type in here."

It's time we start *taking* some of that action.

Ref. *The Last Don* book:

Dante has a "bloody mouth"—that is, he *likes* to kill. One decent hit man went out with Dante on a job said:

"He pants and drools and his hair stands up and a stink steams offen him like a bitch in heat—disgust you to smell it and see it. Won't ever again go out with that Dante, he's a mental."

Bad form, besides he is crazy in his blood. His mother is a real nut case—screaming, breaking plates, lying down and kicking—"one of her fits."

You see, a hit man has to be *cool*. It's just a job.

Suddenly the Mob moves into legit business, like furniture. So a competitor is giving trouble. What we do?

How he like to wake up and see his teenage daughter's head on his bedpost? Maybe then he'll see we is giving the best deal.

Who shot Mutie? She has a pellet in her innards.

Like to get my blackjack onto that face done that.

Keep looking.

March 18, 1997. Tuesday

Called the vet. Pellet is, it seems, a BB. Not recent. No need to remove.

On with *The Last Don*.

I see he is all too ready to overlook dangerous and unnecessary behavior (like cutting someone's prick off, and worst of all he *enjoys* doing it):

"He is growing. He will wisen," the Don says indulgently.

"No, Don, he will not wisen. He will *never* wisen."

In your heart, you know that.

Dante is rotten to the core of Hell. And the sooner the quicker.

"Don, your indulgence of this 'bloody mouth' endangers us all, and stains us with vileness. 'Typical wop trick'—cut off a man's prick, throw acid in a woman's face. He is bad for our image. *La bella figura*."

And what else does a man have?

Nada.

Now. "My Day."

Things Eleanor would never say:

"Tried to persuade Franky to commute the death sentence in a case involving the Lindbergh Law. A stupid criminal had forced a police officer at gun point to take him across a state line. Franky said: 'It had to be an example.'

"Example of what? Of the new law being applied in all its vigor to a minor or marginal offender.

"He said: 'That's ridiculous,' and scooted out of the room in his beastly wheelchair—

"That I have to clean up when he shits himself, you see a nurse or attendant just might talk: 'I cleaned up the President's shitty diaper.'

" 'It would be bad for my image,' he says, and I says: 'Your image is shit with me. Disgusts me to see it.' "

Every Don must have a "bloody mouth" at times, to inspire the fear that they need— if this role can be assigned to someone else.

"He is still young!"

"Well, he shouldn't get much older."

"Please, he is my *son*, from my blessed Cherifa, Puta de Palermo."

"He is your misfortune, and you cannot rub his blood from your hands and your heart, and you cannot deny or evade your blame. You would look proudly in the other direction while your son cuts off someone's prick? and shoves his nuts down his throat? This is not good clean work."

(This is the work of the Untouchable class—in Arabia, the Sollubi. When they got to work with red hot pliers on the wounded, they was quickly outlawed as a deadly and intolerable weapon. In many cases the Bedouins, finding the Sollubi deep in the vilest tortures—fabricating iron pricks and heating them up in little pots, and chuckling and pissing and shitting with the fun of it—couldn't contain themselves, and just waded in with cutlass and pistol and cut the vile Sollubis to Hell.)

"Dante is you in that Sollubi class?"

Gregorio, who had heard this bullshit many times about cosmic processes, said:

"Well you got your earthquake warning. The Family doesn't like it."

Let your pen ride and tell you what you think you don't know.

So why you do this, when it is already too late not to not do. Well?

No answer is asked or not given.

So why not give any answer, if it does not give rise to the other question?

March 18, 19, 1997. Wednesday

They say only love can create, so who the fuck could love up a centipede? He's got more love in him than I got.

Now, killing a centipede makes me feel safer—like, one less.

March 20, 1997. Thursday (First day of spring)

Dream about Jane Bowles last night. She has stopped drinking for one day, and feels ever so much better. A machine measures her "betterness," which glows a satisfied pink, like a contented cow.

"I reckon."

When Old Arch used his pipe, it could be plain panic for fake folk, because you can't hear that sound and lie.

Is there a basic lie in being alive in a body?

Of course. But most folks don't know that.

Start: the Grays scan the area for conflict—friction—*Energy*.

Medley of war, famine, pestilence, hate, fear and death.

Planet Earth. (Nice folk, nice ignorant folk.)

She has this sensitive mission to hybridize an offspring with an Earthling—other experiments had been uniformly unsatisfactory.

March 21, 1997. Friday

Many ex-stars die in semipoverty.

Last Don.

A good biographical anthology would be cases of riches to rags: That famous junky (Deere?) etc.

"Bobby [Bantz] is under analysis to make him more likable."

"Therein the patient must minister unto himself."

What a portrait of National Weakness is the whole concept of psychoanalysis. Again the shifting of responsibility. Introduced by Madison Ave, the movie as entertainment. Words, academics, writers—in fact, the whole sophisticated, informed liberal establishment.

"No, I didn't do it—[it] was my neurotic done it."

Don Clericurzio says:

"Everyone is responsible for everything they do."

Hear! hear!

Drunk or sober, mad or sane.

I enunciate the Doctrine of total responsibility, drunk or sober, psychotic, possessed by the Devil, under any coercion.

Putting one's unsightly self in the hands of a wise old father doctor:

"U is my wicked wabbit

U is my great big Daddy

U is my great big wicked wabbit Daddy."

—on the way to an eventful session.

And [danced] into the doctor's facilities, pleading an attack of dysentery.

(As to whether any patient should be allowed to use the doctor's crapper is a moot point.)

Patient, deep in the vilest transference, leaps into the doctor's lap and pisses all over him, slobbering out infantile endearments:

"U is my icky bicky Daddy—Oh!—I've had an *accident* in my diapers."

Situations arise in therapy that require expert handling.

Hum yes, definitely.

In this case, the therapist must act firmly but in no way that could be construed as paternal. It is a very fine line.

Refuse firmly to change the diapers he has purchased on his way to the office and donned in a subway toilet—where he was traumatized by frantic sex freaks—he is already regressing—

"Go away, you dirty boy. I'll tell my daddy on you."

As it turned out the patient was suffering from Wilson's Disease *and* a brain tumor.

There is a lesson here, all too often ignored: be sure you have exhausted the possibility of any organic disorders before embarking on the perilous seas of in-depth analysis.

In the book, *The Last Don*—a great read.

The Clericurzio [family] should keep a low profile, or they will be swamped with soldier candidates:

They tunnel under the walls, they drop from the sky in parachutes, balloons, hang gliders:

"It is my dream, Don, to work for you as a soldier—please don't judge my courage by my crooked leg." (He has one.)

"Let me show my Don what I can do, Sir. Let me help to pull the Gambinos down a peg."

Now one bursts up through the earth of the vegetable garden:

"I'm no fucking queer, I got no fucking fear, all I got in my heart is loyalty to my Don."

Calling Captain Bligh:

"Clear the enclave of this rabble, Mr. Pippi."

They are coming up through the earth like dragon's teeth, and raining down from the sky. The ominous sound of air hammers as they attack the walls—now the wall crumbles like a bursting dam from the pressure of multitudes.

"And the walls came tumbling down."

The Don appears on his balcony in nautical dress:

"Every man for himself. *Sauve qui peut.*"

A helicopter plucks him from his balcony and takes him to a flying saucer [that] hovers, waiting for him.

He leans out for a moment:

"So long, suckers. I'm off to greener pastures."

Now I had always assumed that only love in its widest context could create life. I can feel myself stroking and loving lemurs, cats, weasels out of the air—

But who or what could stroke a fucking centipede, scorpion, funnel-web spider out of any air and love it?

Perhaps a move to some further foothold on the evolutionary cliff of survival.

"There was no other way on to the snake, the lizard, the furred lizard . . . *Animals! Homo Sap!*"

(Deafening applause)

The centipede exists to remind us of the fall we might have taken, except for that repugnant ledge.

"I want—I want."

Homo Sap was always a greedy ass hole, supplied by his voracious fucking mouth.

You see, the centipede was a step to a snake, a lizard, a furred lizard, an animal. And this is [the] basis for a centipede being rejected more than any rejection: looking down on the fall we might have taken, except for that repugnant, momentary ledge.

For the poor rejected Pede, the ledge was permanent.

"But where is love?"

Remember Bill Wilson. In Tangier empty streets—luckily—and he has opened a knife and is slicing the air, as he screams and sobs:

"Where is love?"

"For God's sake, put the knife away. You aren't likely to find love that way."

Fortresses—like Don Clericurzio's Bronx enclave—were outmoded by artillery, aerial bombardment, biologic and chemical agents like Ebola virus and nerve gas, shot into enclave with a slingshot, lands in the vegetable garden.

Shortly after lunch the Don fell ill. Goes to his room.

When he is not out by five P.M., Diego is disturbed. He knocks, then enters the Don's bedroom.

The Don, his face oozing blood, can barely speak:

"It's a plague. No use. Call doctors."

Twenty-four hours later, the enclave had been quarantined. An unexplained outbreak of the Ebola virus. Mortality rate 80–90%.

It was the end of the Clericurzio family. Surviving soldiers scattered, seeking what employment they could find.

Ironically, the Don's dream was being realized: they were absorbed into the USA, [a] completely disposable unit, now—and this [is] ironic—with the old Don's power.

"The Last Don," indeed . . . remember the *Le Grande Illusion:*

"Don't know who will win, but it's the end for the De Gramonts and the Gottfrieds."

Old families, where the mother said "*vous*" to her sons and never "*tu*"—too familiar—and a true aristocrat can never allow any chink of intrusion into her impeccable image as a warrior.

There is no rule for the confront that must occur here and now—Let it come down.

March 22, 1997. Saturday

All Quiet on the Western Front.

"It's a long way to Tipperary . . . Keep the home fires burning"

—dim, grainy, far away 1917–18—

"But my heart's right there."

Suddenly break through of sound and image—loud and close.

4:50 [P.M.] Allen Ginsberg called, from Beth Israel Hospital. Voice sounded curiously weak. He had hepatitis, wrong experimental medicine (this has happened to him before). Now must rest and cancel all engagements. No trip to Italy, no Naropa, nothing until mid-July, then very important performance date.

Well, there I am in East St. Louis, talking to some old-time short-con gambling Johnson with a slight German accent.

I said: "I'm betting against myself."

They didn't like that very much. An old-timer, years of old rooming houses, chili joints behind him. His eyes were quick and clever, sincere and untrustworthy. For so many years he had to look out for himself.

Wasn't a junky, I can always tell.

So what was his Ace in the Hole?

(A great revival of ACE IN THE HOLE!)

About fifty, back to his furnished $10-a-week *Hole*.

How can anyone endure this furtive, precarious life without junk?

Shows me the full power that junk has over me, lying hypocrite that I am.

"Oh yes, oh yes—I'm off the junk."

Knowing that abrupt withdrawal from Methadone, 60 milligrams per day, would in all likelihood be fatal.

Advice for young people:

"Anything that can be done chemically, can be done in other ways."

Granted sufficient knowledge of the factors involved. But those who seek cheap rewards from nonexistent work will, of course, be disappointed.

Jerry, I quote:

"So I'll just travel and be cruel to people."

(interesting, other pen gave out on "cruel," it just faded out)

Jerry Wallace is dead.

Who lives will see.

I remember a student when I was teaching at [CCNY]—the student wrote:

"I was informed of the contents of this course, so *I was less harmed by it* than I had been by previous (sic) *courses.*" (should be *curses*)

Less harmed!

What a mentality!

Like [Jerome] Lloyd Wallace at his worst, which is indeed atrocious.

(The fade-out would seem to indicate death.)

I suddenly went a bit sour on *The Last Don.* It happens, reading along to the climax—then . . . lose interest. With the Crichton book, they were about to abduct the hero to Tokyo.

Not that the *denouement* is so predictable, *I just don't care*—like energy leaked out of the book.

I am at the last chapter, the Santado War. It's all so *old-fashioned.* These Dons and their intricate feuds and maneuvers.

This, of course, is the breath of life to these tiresome old relics. With their sound opinions and inexorable values and sanctions.

Fold sweet etcetera to bed.

You have lived your life as you saw it, Don Clericurzio, now it is time to rest—with old malaria-ridden English-coasters from West Africa, German Junkers with their tiresome scars from student duels.

Let's have a little comic relief. Here is the student duel:

Starts, and right [away] a sharp cut, it will make a splendid red scar.

Then, his bloody face twisted in a maniacal killing rictor, he slices off the other student's head, clean off. It bounces among the appalled witnesses.

"*Unerhört!*"

"*Er hast die ganze Kopf aufgeschnitten!*"

The body sags to the floor, spurting a fountain of blood.

Any more old relics out there, waiting on disposal?

Any "old men with beautiful manners"?

Any wise old White Hunters?

"Don't ever sell your dream, son, because it isn't yours to sell. It belongs to all mankind."

"I reckon," Arch said.

And there was all wisdom in it.

The Big, Big Reckoning.

Stalin's feared "Enforcer" is dead at 97. Guess he sorta overstayed his welcome.

Any more old doddering has-beens? Fine old has-beens, cutting their coupons?

Who the fuck is "Ernest Vail"— the novelist in *The Last Don?*

"The greatest American writer" . . . a "national treasure," no less.

There isn't any such, even an approximate.

Who? Bill Gaddis? No. There isn't any to come close to Hemingway, Faulkner, Fitzgerald, *Genet, Beckett*—

Look! *Nada!* Nothing. Not even a Kerouac—

I win by total default.

"It just doesn't come anymore."

—as Hemingway mourned and groaned in his last darkening years.

Ultimately, he had no inner fortress, no protection. He never realized that *there is always an enemy,* or we would not be here.

Of course.

"On this checkerboard of
Nights and days . . .
Hither and thither moves
and checks and slays and
one by one back in the
Closet lays."

Rubaiyat of Omar Khayyám

March 23, 1997. Sunday
He suddenly saw and kept seeing what they had been keeping from him all his wretched life.

???

March 24, 1997. Monday

Just put Allen Ginsberg in the Wishing Machine.

His voice over the phone from Beth Israel Hospital in NYC sounded very weak.

(Don't forget to get disposable razors.)

What's the big secret? (above)

The secret is a reliable time-polished device in story, usually reserved for the end, like "the evidence" in Michael Crichton's book about the Salem Witch nonsense.

So where is this wondrous secret they been hiding from him??

There is always an enemy, or we (me and all my relations, rather a select gang) would not be here.

Only thing stirs matter into life, and life into action—lights—camera is opposition on some level (drugs, aliens, child molesters, dissidents . . . and we who must protect ourselves against the idiot reactions of the Moron Majority).

The irritation brings forth culture pearls of common sense. (Above is highly confused.)

Ah yes—perhaps I am a hybrid with an alien.

"*They*" conceal this?

Who are "they"?

The Aliens, of course, and his father—under heavy coercion.

His mother suspects:

"No! no!"

All right, Papa Hemingway. Give us an ultra-short.

Here we are under a tornado watch—and what happens? What event is precipitated by the watch?

(Folks pick through their ruined homes—and after the tornado—a bottle of Absolut, and the sun comes up.)

Look here, Papa.

Now look, it's the time for miracles.

March 25, 1997. Tuesday

It seems that young Dante, grandson of Don Domenico
Clericurzio, has a "bloody mouth"—goes [in] for torture—
started out, as usual, on small animals—instead of a cool quick
job and finished.

The Don disapproves [but] says indulgently:

"He is young. He will wisen."

Every Don, dictator, warlord must show a "bloody mouth" at
times, to bolster the fear they inspire and desperately need. Especially if it is someone else's "bloody mouth"—say, an overzealous
police chief, like Beria. Same formula—and *rumors* of torture,
of traitors being burned alive in crematory ovens. Such rumors
activate archetypical horror and, above all, *fear*. Fear inside.

Trujillo carried fear about with him like another self, almost
visible. His assassins bungled it. They were caught and tortured,
took ten days for them to die. Their bodies ravaged by red-hot
pliers, enemas of sulfuric acid, eyes eaten out by rats, fold sweet
etcetera to bed, were thrown to the sharks.

Trujillo's fear reaches from the grave.

I would have had a list of *all his supporters or suspected supporters or potential supporters*—a long list—and made a clean
sweep of it.

After my sweep (about five hundred to feed the sharks—more
like a thousand), I take over all communications.

Install myself in a fortress, declare a state of emergency, the
bloody lot.

I weed out his name, pull down his statues. No such person ever existed.

He was a malignant mirage, an image of hate.

We are now delivered from his evil old hands, hands of torture and death.

Back to Old Arch:

"You know what happens to old creeps like you, Arch?"

"They is fucked up the ass by the prison population."

"Shit, they line up."

"I reckon," Arch says.

He is pulling a fiddle out of the air.

"Well, some music for the road, feller say."

"Faster faster round and round

swing your partner offen the ground

Faster faster round and round."

On the road back to town, the car with the two Feds in [it] was caught in a "freak wind" and blowed offen the road. The two Feds was pronounced dead at the scene.

March 26, 1997. Wednesday

How's this for an Absolut cartoon: Uncle Sam does a Cossack dance on the *enemies*—drug dealers, child molesters, terrorists, dissidents—with a bottle of Absolut balanced on top of his silk hat.

March 28, 1997. Friday

Two Glasgow boys sit against a wall and mutter:

"No, we didn't say nothing, mate."

Insulting comments on the passersby.

And sometimes a boy will go into what is known as "Dossing," a state where he justs lets [outrage] *flow* through him. A slight [sound] accompanies "dossing." It is a state sought-after and respected by the other boys, who fall into reverent silence in presence of the "Doozing Boy."

> *He loses the Dooz*
> *sooner or later*
> *anything goos*
> *Just keep the Dooz*
> *As long as you can Pose*
> *and hold together*
> *In heavy weather.*

James's horoscope said: "Shocking news this evening," and while we are having dinner (Thursday night), he got a call that John Lee, architect, old friend, has killed himself jumping from a dam at Clinton Lake.

March 30, 1997. Sunday

John Lee apparently killed himself by jumping from the dam at Clinton Lake, sixty feet down to a rock ledge.

"Investigating the death of—relatives on Thursday night— noticed the man's body—into a downtown eatery late last week —One dog's lakeside—There were no obvious signs—Mojo 805VT—"

After the door of foul play was forced open—someone tried again to pry open the cause of death—

Empty all the graves of hanged men. Let their death curse—of the snapping spine, a little "pop" they say—go . . . ejaculate DEATH, *Tod, Muerte, la Mort.*

With this device they could have brought them Boers to their knees, quicker and slicker, because the curse would *work.* The force of a group concentrate is something [will] cut through some Boer Judge with nothing but inherited bullshit to protect him. They rip him to pieces. They garrote him. He's got nothing.

Mayor Bruce McManaway saw group concentration lift a piano into the air. Piano weighed like 300 pounds at least. It was in London.

He gave a very convincing demonstration of White Magic:

"You are going up through a tunnel of light. You will be met by kind guides and friends."

Very nice. Very pleasant.

April 1, Monday, that is March 31, 1997

It will be a Tuesday.

Yesterday went to the service for John Trent Lee. Suicide obviously, but a wedge of doubt. He was a good Catholic, and suicide is destroying the work of God, in Catholic eyes.

But who can say when God turns a blind eye?

How easy it can be—say, for an old-time upper-class English, Eton, Oxford, the lot, everything *so* certain, the bougainvillea, the bungalow—

—for a split second—malaria headache coming on.

He went into the bathroom and took two morphine pills, feeling the pulsing headache pain shift softly to pulsing waves of relief.

Quote Conrad:

"As pain is drowned in the flood of drowsy serenity that follows a dose of opium."

An Outcast of the Islands, Joseph Conrad.

What was it about John Lee?

I never quite believed in his reality. There was something non-existent about him.

The night I spent in his apartment (that later exploded from gas leak, he just made it out in time)—

So I saw him, or I never quite saw him, [from] time to time after that.

Then with the Heidsiecks . . . champagne people [who] were here.

April 2, or environs, 1997

As we near the millennium, Good and Evil slugging it out on this checkerboard of nights and days.

The mass cultist suicide led by the Piper Do. Thirty-nine went peacefully, with phenobarbital washed down with vodka. They were headed for a higher human condition. UFOs, in the wake of the current comet [Kohoutek], would pick them up, once disencumbered of their earthly raiments.

What else?

I must feed the fish.

I have fed the fish.

Like all of us here on planet desperately fluctuating between total chaos and total stasis, the fish exist on a precarious recess.

What ever happened to Faulkner, brother of William Faulkner, who became an elitist Federal Narcotics Agent? Was his brother proud to see a shameless advocate of bureaucratic rule from the Capitol, as opposed to the states'-rights advocates left over from the Civil War?

I imagine they had some arguments:
"Don't you understand? It's a whole different perspective."
"Don't reckon I like this 'different perspective.'"

Come to search my premises. Figure we need a surveyor out here, to determine where my premises is and isn't, or maybe half is and half isn't—a fine line, be sure you keep your eye on the goal.
"Where you desire to be."
    Day is done.
      God is nigh
Or *was* nigh.
The universal Betrayal has swamped the earth.
They look up for mercy like cowering, pleading dogs. Many piss themselves and perform incredible postures of submission—one rushes forward and polishes an official's foot with the oil on his nose.
Official leans back, with a toothpick in his mouth. Then he kicks the supplicant in the mouth, knocking out a tooth.
The supplicant looks up at him and smiles.
"We had use for such revolting beasts for a time. You are no longer necessary."
Such fascist sentiments do not reflect our current colonial policy.
Lines of poetry send ripples—awaiting the sound of a little voice.

Thursday morning, April 3, April 2, Present, 1997

My two most outrageous images—before which the Captain who boards the first lifeboat in drag, the pilot who bails out of a passenger plane leaving the passengers to crash—pale into banality.
Very difficult to describe or even indicate with words.

The first [was] way back, Price Road days. I was driving, and thinking:

"What a terrible thing to run over and kill a child."

Then something emerged, I could feel it coming up from some deep dark lair: a shadowy black figure, carrying a dead child over one arm with indescribable contempt:

"This yours?"

At the University Club in NYC. I saw a spastic waiting for the elevator. He has a crutch.

I see myself push him to the floor, grab his crutch with insanely grotesque drooling and repulsive imitation of his affliction while he flops on the floor like a displaced fish.

(Oh yes, reading le Carré's *Night Manager:* a crippled man limping through tables. He had two walking sticks. His *rhythm* discomfited the diners. That's what lit a powder trail to the spastic in my club.)

The juncture when I might have become a big-time pusher with Mafia backing. My big chance. And I bungled it.

I had to do something else. I am a natural born scribe, a writer.

Two people I want to know where, or if, they are:

Bill Gilmore and Jerry Wallace.

Bill would be 86. May well be deadly.

Jerry? I had a strong feeling he is dead.

I never saw him after the long [1983] tour: Minneapolis, Finland, Norway (two stops), Sweden, Denmark. (When I got back, James's white cat had disappeared.)

Point: I saw him *before* the tour. Since? *Nada.*

Our relationship in Paris doesn't bear looking at, or *après.*

Gilmore always wanted to "write a great book." He went into publicity, and somehow he never got around to writing the "great book."

I want to see him and grind his nose in it: *I wrote the great book.*

Remember [I] went out to dinner with Gilmore and Ilse, New York City, many long years ago.

I was talking about getting in some kinda business, and barkeeper saying:

"Rats! Rats! Rats!"

What kinda friend is this?

Jerry? Well, he's one of the worst, in there with Mary McCarthy's "Young Man" and Walter Ramsay in "Shut a Final Door," by Truman Capote.

And our relationship does not bear close inspection on the surface . . . nothing under the surface.

Room 15, room 18.

"Everyone is responsible for his or her own actions—everything they do."

Don Clericurzio, in *The Last Don.*

He meant to end the Don rule by taking out one family. A very far-sighted and ruthless move.

The Assassins of Hassan i Sabbah did not fear torture. Why not?

A little scrawny man, accused of killing people twice his size and carting away the body. He demonstrates by hefting two-hundred-pound detectives off the floor. He could pick up and carry [them] in his arms—like cables, no flesh in them—but the laws soon tired of *this* game.

"Will they hang you?"

"Oh yes," he answers. "But I won't be there."

The guards put cigarettes to his arms, slapped him.

No use. Had to hang him in a chair. Because he wasn't there.

He was accused of having robbed and murdered a number of citizens, decent fucking citizens.

Another thing about this little scrawny ugly man was his eyes. They lit up inside from time to time, like a furnace door opened and closed in some private special Hell he carried about with him. There was something about those *eyes*, and a musky zoo stink about him.

I saw a picture of him strapped to a chair and being carried to the gallows.

> *They had to hang him*
> *in a chair*
> *Because he simply was*
> *not there—*
> *and the bank bandit*
> *with the sweet voice*
> *"Everybody please*
> *put your hands up*
> *high."*

It was the sweetest voice any bank clerk ever heard. For those who resisted his sweetness and reached for a button:

"He got a terrible gloating feeling when he killed someone." Sounds good to me.

Then it hits—a world without the voice of Allen.

I can feel his voice now—

"Oh, bits and pieces," he says—

getting together in . . .

The aficionado who approaches bullfighters with loathsome passes and snorts of dying bull.

All right.

Still April 3, 1997. Thursday

Allen Ginsberg is dying of liver cancer.

"About two to three months," the croakers tell him, and he says:

"I think less."

He says:

"I thought I would be terrified; instead I am exhilarated."

Just hope he isn't flooded with suffocating endearments.

"Allen is writing poems—he is inspired."

The beginnings of *life came to this planet on comets.*

April 5, 1997. Saturday

Allen Ginsberg died [this morning]; peaceful, no pain.

He was right. When the doctors said 2–4 months, he said:

"I think less."

April 6, 1997. Sunday

"Life"

—a sort of maimed existence known as Your Fun. Gratitude is requested.

"Liberty"

—"Don't take me for dumber than I look"

"And the Pursuit of Happiness."

Pursuit is a promising Chestnut. Gelding Happiness may be a little past prime, but past races to be taken in consideration. She will be ridden by Serenity, a very *experienced* jockey, who recently changed his name to Tedium.

Remember:

"Kerouac back from the grave with a good Catholic prick. I thought Bill would like to know he's passing through town."

This the guy says on tape:

"The fact that you exist is an insult to me."

"Who are you?"

"What did Allen have?"

A basic directness of viewpoint, related to the Indian Monkey God.

Like the young acolyte in search of the Master found that Allen Ginsberg has just left.

What am I talking about?

Old Monet haystacks and Pissarro. My hands in theirs, like loving gloves—led me to those *beautiful* colors.

Splash the young dude in the vest. A handsome type, my dear—

whose dear are *you?*

And where were you when your flight was canceled?

It's against the law.

In those days we had the pick of the young ones, all cute and scrawny.

"I often have seconds," confided a retired English official who patronized the Arab punks.

There were two in Tangier: one the Spanish boy pimp—"Tony the Swede"—and the Arab boy pimp.

Here we are at April 8, 1997

Thirty-two [degrees] outside, cold and windy.

Allen?

So many—

click/Tangier, click/Paris, London, NYC, many clicks.
Los Angeles, City of the Angels—

April 9, 1997. Wednesday

Last night jumbled dream about a $65 suitcase that I had bought
from Fred Baxter, and a girl behind a desk said:

"Can I help you?"

I said:

"Yes—my suitcase, that I paid for in [an] area known as Luxor,
has been stolen."

She says:

"Are you ready to go to a police station to report this?"

I said:

"Yes."

But nothing happened.

After that, trying to find my way back to nowhere in particular . . . an incredible area of streets, [buckled] sheets of glass, laid
flat. Still I look for food.

Where is this $65 suitcase?

Where is Fred Baxter, and who and when and why?

Reeds and water in hieroglyphs for the concept of???

Where is Gregory? In all the publicity about Allen's death.
Where is Gregory?

What is happening?

April 10, 1997. Thursday

Reading *Denial of the Soul,* by M. Scott Peck, M.D. Very good,
very sound, and rejecting the dogmas of psychiatric treatment.

"They" grossly underestimate the role of *Possession,* much more
common than "they" think—if their cerebral process can be so
dignified. Retards, for the most part.

The case of Howard: some entity, organism in his body all the way, did not wish to be evicted—and saw Peck as a deadly danger.

And it would seem to kill the host [by suicide is] the worst danger?

It happens when the beast is cornered.

Not so intelligent, but very purposeful.

"And freedom shall a
while repair
to dwell a weeping
hermit there . . .
gradual dusky veil"

I forget the poet's name.

"When spring with dewy
fingers cold
returns to deck this
hallowed mould!"

"Ou sont les neiges d'antan?"

*"J'aime ces types vicieux
qu'ici montrent la bite."*

"I like the vicious types who
show the cock here."

*"Simon, aime tu le bruit
des pas sur les feuilles mortes?"*

"Simon, do you like the sound of
footsteps on dead leaves?"

I do.

April 10, 1997. Thursday

To Kansas City with Wayne. Very careful driving. Accidents are pandemic because of darkness and rain.

I took a booster dose of 30 mg of Methadone before starting, and 70 mg at the clinic, so I felt fine and had a very unusually good breakfast at Nichols'. My standard for 15 years—two fried eggs straight up, medium, three slices bacon, hash browns, white toast and three cups of coffee.

Where is Jerry Wallace?

In Wichita perhaps. I have contacts.

April 11, 1997. Friday

Just a few memorable expressions:

Vail Ennis, Sheriff of Beeville, Texas:

"They'll talk, or they won't be in a condition to talk, one or the other."

(ref. hold-up suspects):

"[They] think they are tough. I'm not tough. There is no such thing as a tough man."

Same words exactly from a Mafia Don, passed along to me through Little Jack Melody, a surrogate.

[—] means me no good. *He left his umbrella,* a very bad sign, and [an] assassination M.O.

Bastards—remember at Dr. Dent's, the apomorphine M.D.:

"I have to be able to get back in here."

Ref. an umbrella from Paul Bowles.

Door rings. He gets his umbrella and gives me a tape, called "There Comes the Smile."

Maybe I'm—

maybe I've seen too many "umbrellas"—

too many smiles.

He comes back for his umbrella, and gives me a tape, called "There Come the Smiles."
Where exactly?
At who? And why?
Yeah, yeah, I guess he's OK.
But?

Miranda on the veranda
is a sweetheart of mine
from the lack of Miranda
I simply peck and pine
while waiting for my mouthpiece
to put all the pieces in line
Till then my only words are
Miranda on the verander
waiting for my defender
all the children of Miranda
are united in the right of silence.

So one must write what I am and what we both are at last.
You, I see, are ready.
I, too, am ready—
now we become one.
The Apomorphine doctor—you think it cured me?
It doesn't at all.
So where—
You got ten to serve.
Fred Baxter.
He doesn't move in my circles.
He'd just seen his hang-face killer fried in the Chair, and his own hair stood up and *crackled* with joy.

Just [the] other day, a witness to Texas lethal injection: he exulted, raising his arms.

"Was it good?"

"Dear— —

"I have never wroted a fan letter before.

"How many fan letters have you gotten which started with sentence one? I have received a thousand at least.

"My name is William S. Burroughs. I am a humble practitioner of the scrivener's trade, a Tech Serg[eant] in the Shakespeare Squadron, as we called it in the war no one knows about. Except those who were in it."

Old unhappy far-off things, and battles long ago.

April 12, 1997. Saturday

Today I have learned what it *feels* like to turn myself into a Beast. The way the teeth tear through my bloody gums, the hairs sprouting through my flesh and skin like a million hot needles, the claws sprouting from my fingers.

My face is fluid now, it will take any form.

Say 1920 Fitzgerald "radiant boy"—radiant boy in my face now.

Stutz Bearcats outside, it's the 1920s.

More of [a] bore than beast—the old warmed-over winter dreams, so tattered and torn and frayed by the tiny mouse-bites of time.

What once glowed with the fire within
now sputters out puffs of—of—

What once glowed
now sputters—
The Beast is now. The radiant boy of the 1920s is then.
Dear dead days—*ou sont les nieges d'antan?*
Where are the snows of yesteryear?
The Beast eats from within. It's very painful. Writhing, screaming, growling, snarling, grunting beast pain.

Back to my letter to Scotty Peck, M.D.:

"I have never written a fan letter before.

"How many fan letters have *you* got that started out like that?

"Well, Scotty, let me introduce myself—though I think that we have known each other for a long time. My name is William Seward Burroughs, a humble practitioner of the scrivener's trade—a Tech Serg[eant] in the Shakespeare Squadron, in the war nobody knows about except those who were in it, when the whole shithouse was about to go up.

"(Wheels turn in one's head—paranoia—brilliant intellect, deadly dangerous.)

"We agree on so many points. I *detest* secular humanists, like the *Skeptical Inquirer*. Objective they are not.

"Three times I wrote on their impudent paper to me:

"'Anyone denies ESP hasn't kept his eyes open.'

"(None so blind as he who will not look.)

"Three times, before they get the message.

"As a morphine addict off and on, mostly on, for 50 years, I certainly approve your stand on painkillers."

Withdrawal in a precinct cell can occasion both physical and emotional pain, and adequate M.S. is indicated.

My lawyer got me over to a hospital for a shot, ½ grain M.S.

What a difference a shot makes. Not for nothing it is known as "God's Own Medicine."

"Twenty milligrams, quarter-grain!"

Echoes down the halls.

Half-grain—more to the point.

April 12, 1997. Saturday

"Half a grain, G.O.M."—echoes down the hall.

Where are they?

Where are Pat and the others who are supposed to fix my dinner?

I can hardly write anymore. I know this sounds like a last message [from] a space capsule.

Well it is, and I can't do anything more at this point.

No, no

don't think—

no

April 13, 1997. Sunday

I was just saying:

"My energy is at its lowest ebb between 12 and 2 P.M."

—when [I] picked up book I am reading to the phrase:

"at its lowest ebb."

Can I ever catch up with where, on some level, I am?

Reading *Denial of the Soul,* by Scotty Peck, M.D. Very sound. Very good.

Like *The Last Don*—so many dictums of the old Don hit my home. He believes in God. Me, too.

He says:

"Everybody is responsible for everything they do."

Yes, indeed.

And denial of responsibility is pandemic—read Truman Capote's "Shut a Final Door" for the terminal stage of such denial.

He says:

"Never kill a policeman."

Brion Gysin said exactly the same words in room 32, 9 rue Git-le-Coeur.

I feel woozy, like I may be dying—

Who lives will see. Way I feel now, don't know whether to call a doctor or the undertaker. It isn't good.

Fortunately, my *copains* are gathering.

This may be it.

"Seeing that death, a necessary end, will come when it will come."

Shakespeare, *Julius Caesar*.

Any case, no fear—I could die tonight.

I had the real dying feeling an hour or two ago.

It will return, and heavier—

April 15, 1997. Tuesday

Last night sex dream of Marker. Ran my hands down a lean young male body.

Woke up feeling good.

April 16, 1997. Wednesday

Appointment with Dr. Orchard for the cataract operation on right eye on Monday, April 21. Done in Same Day Surgery.

Everyone says I am doing the right thing, and I concur. No anxiety, full confidence in Dr. Orchard and the hospital facilities at Lawrence Memorial. Went there today to fill out forms, give history.

Should have done it sooner. Standard operation, finish and back home in a few hours.

Just finished reading *Denial of the Soul,* by Scott Peck, M.D., a psychotherapist who—like me—believes in God. Very sound book.

In favor of Hospice, as much morphine as is needed to control pain.

He deplores—moderately—secular humanism. So do I—immoderately.

It's got no depth to it. No *elán.* No mystery, no pilgrimage. To these dreamers, there is no place to pilgrim to. No spiritual—I mean, spiritual advancement possible.

April 18, 1997. Friday

Last night dream of Ian, sort of sexy. He was dressed in a most peculiar coverall, including a helmet of some plastic-like brown fabric—perhaps the indestructible material found at Roswell, New Mexico.

Cover-ups are coming fast. Now it seems [TWA] Flight 800 was downed by a missile.

And what is this war on marijuana about? A beneficent drug with no harmful side effects. Why?

There is purpose here, and clearly the purpose needs to be covered up, because it is bad.

I mean Evil. Evil covered by transparent lies, that only the very stupid will believe. And [that] the liars and promoters of the Big Lie work tirelessly (since they have nothing else to do) to promulgate.

People in the mainstream are actually getting stupider, under a deadly hail of lies and misinformation from those in power.

Good God, why ban the medical use of Cannabis—increases appetite, removes nausea, expands awareness: I am in a blind alley—a few whiffs, and I can see five or six ways to write on.

Snide old George Will:

"*Howl* written on benzedrine," etc.

And what, may I ask, are "American values"—or Japanese values, or German values?

To understate the implicit confusion—"over-determined"—having more than one cause.

Our values are legion. High among which are money and power.

Power to extradite citizens of other countries to face drug charges here.

[I'd] like to see Japan extradite the President for retroactive conspiracy to drop the atom bomb, or Honduras to extradite the CIA head on drug-smuggling charges, or J. Edgar Hoover (God rot his soul) seized by his "touch-of-the-tar-brush" and returned to Saudi Arabia or Zaire or Nigeria to face serious sex charges, including transvestitism—and witnesses subpoenaed from Washington and New York.

Confusion will wright—or write—her or his masterwork.

Meanwhile, we must face the fact that our leaders are certifiably insane or worse.

Allen Ginsberg was the first to stand up before Midwest fraternity audiences and talk explicit homo-sex. The boys realized that "there was a God in him."

A God of the search for the *real thing.*

"How dull it is to pause, to make a rest . . . not to shine in use."

"*That*" fades forever.

There is still time to seek a farther shore. The search is as much an American Value as the dreary work ethic by which so many underprivileged Americans live and die. More, in fact, since "the frontier" is a basic factor in American values.

Now that the geographic frontier is gone, there remains the greatest frontier of all: the frontier of space, inner space of the mind and spirit and soul.

Outer space of the astronaut. Let us have more money spent on the space program, and less on the idiot war against drugs, on armaments.

But what chance now does a young man have to participate?

At the time of Columbus a wave of exhilaration swept the Old World:

"It is necessary to travel. It is not necessary to live."

One hoped for such a wave after the first moon shots.

But instead, cover-ups.

"Dangerous"—dangerous to whom exactly?

Where they come from? Why they come from there to here?

Who the fuck are they any case? What they fucking want?

Why they won't talk to the very few intelligent occupants of this planet?

You see what is wrong with Cannabis? It is an *illegal drug.*

And who made it illegal? And why?

Because Cannabis enables one to *see* those who, for very good reasons, do not want to be seen for what they are: enemies of the mammalian race.

What can one do?

Collaborators, like George Will, say:

"Nothing."

The Invaders have it all sewed up tight.

Maybe—*qui vivre verra*—

Who lives will see—

and none so blind as he *who will not look*.

The Invaders are weak. A terrible weakness, counting on a terrible stupidity of the human mainstream. Look at witch burnings, etc.

You just have to keep the Old Fires burning.

No trouble, no energy. No energy, no life.

April 19. Saturday

1:45 P.M. The technical people are here to record Jim Morrison.

Just finished recording. Takes it out of me, and onto the tape. Ten thousand \$ for two hours' work. Hard work, but I enjoy doing a job I can do, and doing it right.

First question about a job is: can I do it and do it right? If not, forget it.

Second question:

"There is the question of my fee."

Nice people. Know their biz as sound engineers. Professional.

Gertrude Stein said, and I agree: the worst misfortune to a man is his failure to find a *métier*—something he does professionally. A trade, a profession.

I am a writer. A scribe. Also, a Priest—like all true scribes.

Deeply spiritual, I detest Bible Belt Christianity—dead, suffocating under layers of ignorance, stupidity and barely hidden bigotry and vicious hate.

Holy-roll away from me!

The Catholics:

"I want to talk about life after death, Father, and the nature of God."

"Best not to think about things like that. Can lead to confusion. And now, I am late to a golf appointment with the Bishop. Remarkable old man, still sharp as a tack."

"Can I arrange to consult the Bishop?"

"'Fraid not, old sport, he's tied up solid from here to Eternity."

"How's about doing a sweat lodge? Lame Deer is in town."

"Oh, I think not."

He edges out the door.

"God, anyone?"

I am not a Secular Humanist. I regret all factors that created this dismal creature known as a Secular Humanist.

I believe in God.

Not omnipotent. He needs help now.

You co-creators, get in there to resist the idiotic and evil War Against Drugs. The people back of this nonsense are basically evil, as far as the human potential is concerned. They have infected [the] planet with an idiot fear, like the witch-hunts of the Middle Ages.

Remember the Congress[ional] messenger in South Africa, who lunged across the table with a Fairbarn dagger (double-edged killing knife distributed to commandos) and stabbed the old creature many times.

Enough.

And what do you know? Whose picture was on the front cover of (James called) *Time* at the time? None other than Verwoerd, then Prime [Minister] (at a ripe age), and look[ing] very unwell, too.

And who succeeded him? The Minister of Defense and Internal Security.

Ho hum—fold sweet etcetera to bed.

April 21, 1997. Monday

Monday. Cataract operation by Dr. Orchard.

Practically painless. Patch on eye. May not read.

Tuesday, patch off.

(Meet old shooting buddy, John Healy, from the [city's] basement [gun range], there to have his patch off.)

There is a Sudlow in the waiting room. Sudlow, the waiting-room artist. Strictly landscapes. Mostly Autumn or Winter. He moved in when I moved out of the Stone House, where that sorry bastard Panta Rhei, né John Tyler, was my landlord. Like many landlords, he hates everybody. Said I was a reprobate breaking down morals.

Ho hum. Reprobate—old-fashioned word—

Reminds me of Charlie Van Southerland, great St. Louis reprobate and—

"Oh, he was charming."

That—I leave it blank—incompetent Doctor Senseney.

"Humph," his wife grunted. "I didn't think he was so charming last time I saw him on the Olive Street trolley. He burped for ten blocks, still burping when we got off."

How the mind burbles—like rotten weeds.

Sure I can read, the doctor says.

But I can't read. He should know.

April 22, 1997. Tuesday

Patch off. Schedule of eye drops.

"Can I read?"

"Yes," the doctor says.

But when I get home, I find that I can't read.

The semantic and grammatic error is mine: I should have said, "May I read?" And the whole condom would have fallen into place. I can only plead post-operative confusion.

Early Thursday morning, terrible nausea—but nothing solid. Took 30 mg Methadone. When James arrived I felt quite well.

Nice chat with Linda:

"Morphine is for pain. So who should get it? People with pain."

April 26, 1997

So it's all mental? All in your head—or is it?

Get to a *neurologist*. Any creep ask me any psych questions— (My cousin died on the couch, of a brain tumor.)

Scuttle back to old *Wien,* like the ghosts you are. Born and died with the Herr Professor Freud.

I complain my fingers don't do always what I tell them anymore.

And he looks at me with low cunning and says:

"Perhaps you have guilty feelings about what your fingers do? *Nicht wahr?*"

Wrong address.

Test reflexes.

Do Scat Tan, I mean Cat Scan.

My reflexes is shot. Can't roll a joint.

Get to the bone of it, Doc.

"Well we need to do some more tests. So far everything is within normal limits. Need to do a spinal tap and—"

Stop.

Maybe it *is* all in my head, the way it was with my cousin in 1920. Bond salesman who suddenly started to puke and suffered [an] attack of . . .

"So you will regurgitate the whole life, *hein?*"

"So you shit on the rules laid down by your father, *hein?* And you run so to the *Mutter* to change your diapers, *hein?*"

The doctor crouches above the couch like an evil gnome, his face twisted into an unsightly grimace of shrewdness and crazed *Menschenkenntnis* (Man-knowledge). He has seen it all. He is, after all, a physician—already covering his ass:

"I assumed, of course, that a neural examination had been performed to the most deep—"

Fortunately the tumor was in any case inoperable.

He is, after all the nonsense, a physician, and what he sees now is a massive hemorrhage and death.

God rest those Dear Dead Days.

Ask my bond salesman cousin, Robert [Hoxie]—who had the misfortune to die before the halcyon days of malpractice could enrich his survived-by's.

It was all in his head.

But that was long ago
and now my inspiration
is in the tar dust
of the sty.

Last night dream some.

So I reckon that was the first thing—after the other things happened, had to happen, could[n't] help happening, and then there was the white road to nowhere and the small fish pool—

Why this pressure from the Feds on pot? A beneficent substance. Why?

April 28, 1997. Monday

Sight always better. What a great decision!

George Wedge stopped by with some *Cottonwood Review*s for me to sign.

Vale was here last night.

I find myself knocking myself out to be charming, and how I love it—to see the subject glow in response. It's a great feeling, that I have only experienced in the last few years. Putting out charm and watching it hit.

This [is] completely different from the fear hit, putting out fear and watching it hit and twist in a cold sore.

I want people to feel better after a meeting, not worse.

Remember Mark, the old clothes dealer in Tangier? Liked to bring someone down a little.

Was Dr. Brunquist really a doctor in Egypt?

"Where [did] you get your degree?"

What business of his, whether he was a doctor or not?

I am "a *kindly* ruin," say the uninvited Boys who aroused [me] from [my] siesta.

The purring fish, the plumed serpent with round, intelligent eyes—

Of course Man was designed to mate and produce offspring from the other animals on the planet.

Instead they cower in the suburbs:

"Don't get mixed up in it, John."

Sorry, baby, you is already mixed up in it, [up] to your cunt.

Far away. Long ago.

It seems I am just coming of age at the age of 83.

Recall coming across a bridge in Vancouver, age 79: all shyness, ineptness, fear of exposure suddenly fell from me.

Chunks of old disabilities falling away, but—
"Too old"
—Panama jukebox.
Marlene Dietrich and Rosemary Clooney?

"I entertained a man I know,
The moon was high and the lights were low.
He said 'I'd like to play a theme,
But its time to drink my Ovaltine.'
He's getting too old
He's too old to cut the
mustard any more
He's getting too old
He's getting too old
He's too old to cut the
mustard any more."

April 29, 1997. Tuesday

Reading *Extinct*, by Charles Wilson.

This Megalon, a super Great White, thought to be extinct for five million years at least. But it has been lurking in the deepest troughs of the ocean, and coagulating some millions of years of deep-sea, no-light smarts.

So they emerge and have the ability to control the minds of men, and to persuade them that their whole mission and duty in life is to *feed the sharks*.

All livestock and fish catches are fed into deep trenches, where sharks are backed up, mouths gaping, heads out of the water.

My sympathies are with the sharks. Suppose they do eat a few people?

Too many people already.

April 30, 1997. Wednesday
Tomorrow May Day, international distress signal.

M'aidez—

"Help me—a great white just etted my better half."

So?

Rarely felt so low. Nauseous, sub-acute. Dull headache.

What's the use in going to a doctor? Vitamin pills and of course tests.

Wouldn't it be great, as Scott Peck suggests, if all medical students had to undergo the symptoms and *feeling* of a spectrum of illnesses. From acute infections to terminal cancer—and Kuru, the laughing sickness. Just a month for each exposure, controlled of course, and a good heavy dose of *excruciating pain*. So they'll know what that feels like.

Course will turn out some very perceptive diagnosticians, and if the student (at any age) does not measure up, he or she will be sent back for a refresher course—of rabies, for example, or meningitis, so he doesn't [mix] it [up] with a headache fake[d] by an addict. Or if he considers a quarter grain of morphine every four hours adequate medication for rabies.

And refreshers for all who undermedicate for pain. Got a whole contingent there in the East Wing. When the wind is right you can hear them screaming from here.

The D.S. listens and smiles:

"As they sewed, so do they reap."

The doctor who prescribed no morphine, five milligrams of Valium or nothing for a painful and terminal cancer, is beginning to get the message:

"I'm a doctor, goddamn it, let me out of here."

"Verily, doctor, you shall not go hence until you have paid the utmost farthing. Would you like your *oral* Valium now, or later?"

The doctor stares straight ahead.

"I always thought patients wanting pain relief were usually fakers, and if not, weak sisters."

"Let's see, you're at seven now. Perhaps we can put it up to 'excruciating.'"

Odd thing, some subjects escape from pain at this point. They transmute pain to pure charge, they *glow*.

Where is this place, calling doctors to judgment?

Well, call it Purgatory or Life Review.

The healing of past trauma is proportional to the vividness with which the trauma is reexperienced.

The dreariness of so many neurotics. They think the universe centers around their stupid problems.

Recall Doctor Kurt Eissler, M.D., now and again said something meant something. He said:

"These intellectual Jews can do anything."

Which I was thinking at the time.

He even said he thought I might be a Saint.

"If you could enter into a warm human relationship with the therapist."

He's got it. $10 an hour.

Not fair, but what is fair?

No, I do not shrink from the Jew shrink.

It's just—

"He wasn't able to help me."

Was he an observing Jew? And what was he observing?

"How can this so-called 'warm thing' be manifest, when I talk and you don't? Tell me *your* dreams, doctor."

At this moment, 5:04 P.M., I have an intense vivid feeling of Allen's presence.

Outside in the leaves. I see him clear. He is playing on unknown instruments, some sort of Cowboy song.

"Are you conscious, Allen."

"Yes. But barely."

Cold shallow breaths.

"Allen come in please—sad, empty here. Allen, what is here?"

"You never loved anybody except your cats, your Ruski and Spooner and Calico . . . Mother, Ian, Brion, Antony Balch?"

Blue sky, far as the eye can see—blue, blue.

Make up a lot of stories of course.

May 1, 1997. Thursday

Mayday

I'm going into my "beast act."

A juvenile delinquent on his way to be deceased has tortured a cat to death in my presence.

While two others held [my] arms.

Now it starts down in [my] belly—a red tide coming up [my] spine. Great canines tear through [my] gums, dripping blood and saliva. Claws race down [my] arms to fingertips, breaking out, quivering.

With a feline twist, [I] shake off the guards.

Now the Chief takes a look, screams and turns to run. He doesn't get far.

The Beast jumps on his back, pulling him down, reaches around and claws the eyes out, down to the throat, a strangled cry—coughing gobs of blood as The Beast rides him to a sewer ditch and shoves his face, or what is left of it, down into the brown water.

Good job and all.

May 2, 1997. Friday

This morning at the bank for a closing.

"You are old, father William."

Eye clearing. What a miracle!

"Let us squeak of important things," said a fat rat: "God, the family and Shakespeare."

Death and the human rendition.

In a tattered brown djellaba, in the café opposite Café Central in the Socco Chico. With a dirty card with my name on it.

He snarls from a tractor as he backs it toward me. That was in Pine Valley, Texas. Nearest town [to] Cold Springs.

And the Jew who runs a hardware store:

"What's eaten you?"

The question turns his face black with hate, black blood streaming from cuts made by a broken pop bottle.

"You're a real *bad* actor," I tell him. "Get some new lines."

"Who put the cyanide in the Tylenol?"

And more crucial, why did he or she stop? The possibilities are breathtaking.

All over the country, he leaves the prepackaged parcels of death—string beans, steaks, aspirin, vodka, sugar—cyanide, botulism, arsenic, aconite, barium—going off like time bombs. Every store needs special security, searches at the door.

Then the sleepers start coming in from the Government Sections. (A club of ortalon Eaters died under their napkins, inhaling the heady almond smell of hydrocyanic acid, cunningly concealed in the greasy heaven of ortalons. Some said they got their just desserts. Keep an open mind, me.)

Some rare old wines and superb Napoleon brandies convey the tingling numbness of aconite:

"My god, I've been poisoned."

"There are certain things which my gut may safely be presumed to know."

Oh, and the Destroying Angels that creep in with the morels and the truffles.

And to revert to the common touch, Hamburgers are no longer Heaven, but a super-tamper with the wholesale meat—to insert scopolomine, LSD, and as final solution, Deadly Nightshade. Subject becomes disoriented, wandering in the traffic with no perception of danger, falling in seizures and fits. Thousands all over the McDonald's, greasy pizza joints, outskirts of any town in the U.S.A.

Well now, there's a scene worth making, *hein?*

But it stopped. Why?

Think with, say, six like-minded accomplices. Maps on the wall. The machines set up to produce labels, the pre-tampered product stands ready.

Now with briefcase, shopping bag, suitcase, the messengers of Death disperse. . . .

They have not yet reached the biologic stage of bleeding fevers, etc.

Great shimmering citadels of my will.
    But, monster of your will, what profit have you?
    The profit of making my own profit.

May 3, 1997. Saturday

The caviar arrived.

I can imagine someone bankrupting himself buying best Beluga at $28 an ounce. He comes home one day, and his fifteen-year-old daughter and [a] bunch of teen chums are eating his Beluga and washing great gobs of it down with milkshakes.

"Come on in and join the party, Pop." Holds up an empty jar: "Too late."

He would have killed them all, had he not dropped down dead for the *Timely* Want of Caviar.

"The workers had to stand in line for a lousy dollar a day."

"You can't scare me, I'm sticking to the union."

"There are no neutrals there,
you'll either be a union man
or scrounge for J. P. Blair."

(Synthetic folk songs concocted by bearded Jews in lofts.)

"'I never died,' said he."

"Where's your proof?"

"From San Diego down to Maine
in factory, mine and mill
where working men defend their rights
'tis there you'll find Joe Hill.
Now the National Guard,
They are a stalwart band.

A lousy bunch of pimps and queers
the finest in the land.
Which side are you on, soldier,
which side are you on?"

Just finished a book called *Extinct*, about Megalons. Great white [sharks], a hundred feet long. Intelligent too.

They have my sympathy. I hated to see that noble fish twenty-five feet long killed by dynamite.

So it ate a few humans? Too many in any case.

But what were they eating down in the deepest trench?

My sympathy is always with the shark. At least the shark is sincere and honest with his intentions, whereas Homo Sap conceals himself behind veils of evasion, as he or she dances an unsightly can-can.

Someone long ago starts singing this:

"Temperature's rising, it isn't surprising, she certainly can Can-Can."

James Le Baron Boyle said later of her singing:

"Too much of a bad thing."

So when were you not there before?

What? It was a short time after.

"Much too short to walk, for a man qualified like you."

The new Boss of Bosses.

"If you refuse, protection you may have taken for granted is abruptly removed."

Servants, maitre-d's snarl at him.

May 3, 1997. Saturday

At twenty-five minutes before seven on a Saturday evening, May 3, 1997.

Writing is such a awkmarked procedure.

"I dreamed you were *eating* my back, from above and over."

Smell of coal gas and dread always closer.

What?

"Swear to God, I done it then and I'll do it again."

The Majority?? Convince or kill. No safe middle ground is possible.

C or K.

Bass, outlaw shot by old Seldman at four feet. Died four hours later. He, that bum outlaw, had killed a decent young ranger for saying he should go home and sober up. Which he finally did, in the back room of a whorehouse, where Bass breathed his last.

Sunday, May 4, 1997.

As he turns the corner, the sea wind gave him a blue blast of hope.

Just a whiff, will he ever get more?

Not if they can help it. What a bore.

Stop it.

Think all over the world, the trillions of people all eating, fucking, sucking, sleeping, dreaming, hoping and what hope can there be in this prison?

A.J. [Connell]?

"He was a very minor prison official."

Some status in being a prisoner, if one knows he is one.

Trained and born idiots are there to scream:

"Paranoia!"

"Woman loather!"

Vile entities twisting about, like *The Temptation of St. Anthony.*
Demons pulling at his beard, trying to keep him from being a
Saint, which he can't help. The impasse inspires these demons,
creatures of energy concentrations, give them the power to touch
and pinch and pull.

Shall I write a bestseller on Doctors I have known?

All my analysts clinging to their dying faith.

Now look, you get a break there, like the first open-heart surgery. Then you go on from there, see? Now it's routine surgery.
So where is their wondrous analysis going on to? Answer:

"Nowhere in particular."

About coming out on Methadone:

"You tell the truth, you can't buy a gun or drive a car. But
nobody wants to open that. You'd be surprised at some of the
names on that Methadone list."

America is full of bureaucratic impasses ready to explode, spray-
ing child molesters and dope fiends across the lawns of suburban
America . . . respectable men in mackintoshes:

"Want some candy, little girlie? Come closer."

Missed that one, getting old. She bit me, hard.

Always cuff 'em hard first, knock 'em half-senseless *before* you
grab 'em. Cupped hands to the ears works well, or a punch to the
side of the throat—[vein] pulses there in terror as you hit him hard
in the stomach:

"Little shit!"

"Now, son, when a man gets on the Beluga Caviar, well, there's
nothing he won't do to satisfy the Caviar hunger eating at his bread-
basket. He'll lie, he'll cheat, he'll even kill for a gob of it. They get

where they aren't even humans anymore. Just vessels for the vile Russian Trojan whore, deploying their deadly cargo."

Allen died April 5, 1997.

May 5, Monday, 1997.

If a plague should or will kill a third of the population, I can only pray that it affects not only humans but domestic animals, with special reference to dogs and cats. The picture of trillions of dispossesed cats is too horrible to be confronted.

"Clutter the glind!" screamed the Captain of Moving Land.

The Methadone clinics emerged in a fog of lies, as one of the early doctors explained to me:

"If we had used the word 'morphine,' we could never have gotten 'official approval.'"

Which illuminates the mind level of "official approval," guided by purely semantic considerations.

Methadone is the first completely successful synthesis of the morphine molecule. Three times the strength of morphine by weight. Five milligrams of Methadone equals fifteen milligrams of morphine, and at some point quantitative factors become qualitative.

Conditions morphine does not alleviate (leprosy of the eye, venom of the Stone Fish) could perhaps be controlled by Dilaudid, Heroin or Methadone, in injectable form.

As could be foreseen, this magic cure for heroin addiction is equally addictive. I know. In Tangier I had a two-year habit on injectable—[biseptom] or whatever name—methadone, which is just plain junk.

Like I say, a pyramid of lies.

Like this magic elixir to keep off whiskey is to drink a lot of gin.

Now take some sex offender. He's done his time, put all that behind him, but boys shout at him:

"Sex criminal! Short eyes!"

And pelt his trailer with stones.

He looks up at the wall, where a curio Kris from a Marine buddy is mounted.

He stood up and felt the red tide come up from his gut and blow through the top of his head.

"I'm coming!"—he screamed, as he pulled the door open and leaped out, the Kris vibrating in his hand as those before [him cringe] back—too late, as he hacks and thrusts, his face blank as a porcelain mask.

May 7, 1997. Wednesday

A stone bounced off his forehead, the Kriss turned like a dowser's wand, he dropped to a crouch and sprinted forward. The stone-throwing youth turned to run, stumbled. The killer straddled him, grabbed his hair, pulled back, and the Kriss stroked his neck. And blood spurted out—

(Like I saw it happen once in N.M. when they cut the throat of a goat at Los Alamos [Ranch] School, where they shot friendly badgers. These are valuable lessons. A.J. confides in me: "I was saying to Hitchcock"—the Latin teacher—"just the other day, 'I wonder if they know what they are getting here?'")

The others were gone now, in a wild panic. The police surround the trailer.

Once again the door flies open, and he streaks toward the police line through a hail of bullets. He stops, reverses his grip and throws the Kriss with his last pulse of energy, and the Kriss catches a fat cop in the hollow of his throat, in to the hilt. Another volley and he falls, [his] face "blank and pitiless as the sun."

End of my Penny Dreadful for the day.

"Platicamos un poco."

He asks for a short human reprieve from a coupling basically cold and alien.

"We've got a problem," said Fraser, the villanous attorney in *The Third Pandemic,* quite an interesting story.

I could think of another:

These Elitists get together in a conspiracy to fuck the planet. They have their deadly agent, and they have the antidote.

"So let the useless trillions perish at the Earth Gates? Hummm."

"Sure, the price on the antidote jets through the stratosphere, but who is now left to buy this wondrous anti-serum? Way I see it, we feed it out slow, let folks get a look at the magnitude of the problem. Meanwhile, we at Uni-Labs are struggling with super-human devotion to find the anti-plague. Here at last, but it isn't exactly cheap."

And it little profits that an idle King—

How dull it were to pause, to make a rest, not to shine in use.

Book title: *All the Evil Old Men*—like Fitzgerald's *All the Sad Young Men.*

Cactus Jack Garner: "A whisky-drinking, poker-playing evil old man."

And there was in Iran (I quote *Time*, "The Evil Mullah and the Weak Shah") this evil old mullah, could turn the riots off and on.

Stalin? He never understood evil. He was a cruel, stupid, bigoted, callous peasant, but Evil? No.

Hitler comes much closer. There is one photo where pure Evil just leaks out of him, like incontinence—leaks out around the edges of the photo. If I could find it now.

Bugsy Siegel, with his brutal, handsome, nasty face. Shot through the head at close range with a .30-.30. Through [the] window, as he read his *Evening News*.

So these computer whizzes draw up an Identikit of what [the] next pandemic will look like, and where it will come from.

So books do exactly that—show us where present policies are taking us.

Let me off.

Well, it looks like your number is up, Burroughs.

Way it looks from here.

Look: it's a sharp Hopper out here, just a suburban street, trees, a road, as always, to nowhere; air long gone, nothing here now.

Allen's worldwide influence toward openness, *glasnost*, is unprecedented. He, with the courage of total sincerity, charmed and disarmed the savage Fraternity Beasts.

May 8, 1997. Thursday

Consider crimes that are defined by a *state of being*, rather than the perpetrating of some definite act at definite time and place. Such laws are already in action. In New Orleans I saw the beginning:

Agent: "I'm going to have you sent to prison."

Suspect: "Why Mr. Faulkner?"

(Yes, he was a narcotics agent and a brother to William Faulkner, the Nobel Prize–winning writer. Was he proud of his Fed Revenooer brother? I hope not.)

Suspect: "Why, Mr. Faulkner?"

Agent: "Because you are a goddamn drug addict."

His crime is a state of being, not a criminal act.

I was in the patrol car. I witnessed this interchange, but its full significance was not clear to me at the time.

Now, I can see people arrested because they *are evil and giving out* evil waves.

Might start with Faulkner.

Are you still alive, Faulkner? You have changed sides it seems: to the Central Govt. in Washington, in complete control with thought police, like *1984*.

But a turn of the coin reveals real Being-Criminals . . . B.Cs. They disrupt any office force, expedition, any common endeavors.

What do they do? They just are. L. Ron Hubbard called them "suppressive persons." He was one himself. Always accuse others of doing what you are doing.

Reading *The Third Pandemic:* a malignant resistant strain of psittacosis, parrot fever, with a deadly incubation time of two to three weeks, during which the subject can communicate his disease and send other infective agents to spread the news.

> *"Is it not fine to*
> *Dance and Sing*
> *While the bells of*
> *Death do ring?*
> *Turn on the toe*
> *Sing out Hey Nonny No"*

"If I should die, think only this of me: there is some corner of
a foreign field that is forever—"

Tangier—Mexico, D.F.—St. Louis, Mo.—Paris—London—
New York City—202 Sanford Ave, Palm Beach, Fla.—Lawrence,
Kans., at this address, 1927 Learn Hard Ave.—and a soupçon of
Athens, Albania, Dubrovnik and Venice—

Releasing such a vile stench of unconsummate, [tripped]-up
affairs . . .

So why bother?

"You are old, Father William.

So why stand on your head?"

These factors [weigh]—

What was, I mean, was what?

A question in Egyptian glyphs: a reed in water.

May 8, 1997. Thursday

Clinic day. Teresa at the take-out slot.

Nice breakfast in Waid's.

Paté came. American Caviar came. Not as good as the Russian but much cheaper, from American sturgeons.

Back to Cousin Bob and his inoperable brain tumor, the psycholo-
gist covering his Viennese ass:

"I assumed, *natürlich,* the needed nervous checks had been
made to the bottom most deep."

May 9, 1997. Friday

What do I have for short-pieces book?

1. Young Man, Shut a Final Door
2. Paul Swann

3. Snarling gunman
4. Señor Kaposi
5. —

May 10, 1997. Saturday

Why didn't James come by to take me to Eudora to pick up my S&W .22, 8½ oz. model 317? Couldn't reach him on the phone all day. The arrangement was definite. So *warum?*

"For he was a doctor
Brave and true?
He killed all the patients
That came within his [view]
And he looked around
For more when he was
Through."

So—dreams that I cannot recapture—flashes—

In a plane landing in a city street on precise alignments. I can see the attic windows under slate roofs, all gray and 1920. Will the plane crash?

And here is Maurice Girodias, looking younger. I must be in the L.O.D.

Lakes, swimming pools, always water—

Where is James, at 4:57 P.M.?

Well, Pat will take me tomorrow morning.

Sunday, May 11, 1997, 11 A.M.

Pat Connor—the O.R. personnel watch, appalled, as he pulls a crude rubber valve from his pocket.

"I am the doctor," he announces, as he slams the valve home.

Went out to Fred's and shot very well with my new eye.

("'Eye, Eye, Sir,' said the Ensign.")

This then is a Monday.

It was a Monday when Jesse James was shot by Ford:

"The dirty little coward
Who killed Mr. Howard
And laid Jesse James
In his grave."

Now Fred opened a saloon in Colorado. Had trouble with this ex-cop. Cop walks into his joint in the morning. Fred foolish[ly] goes out without a gun. Cop shoots him and kills him.

It was a Monday, May 12, 1997

That sorry bastard fat poulter pigeon Newt Gingrich, belching out a death sentence for dope dealers, *ETC*.

Just another sorry, stupid, bigoted windbag.

"For a politician's will is the wind's will,
and their thoughts is wrong, wrong thoughts."

He's no decent little newt.

May 12, 1997. Monday

A long time ago, but not too far to walk.

Remember in the dream I was young, with all life ahead of me, in an 1890 small town, full of nice folk. Nice ignorant folk.

I wasn't in any hurry. Silver dollars jingling in my jeans. Back when a dollar bought a feast of a meal, with fresh walleye and grouse and venison, *and a real steak* (now an endangered or extinct species). Washed down with the best French vintage—oh yes, and of course, best Beluga caviar to start—with ice-cold vodka.

Or [a dollar] could buy you a good piecea ass. Any size, race or color.

So where did we go wrong?

Well, I figure the wrongness was always there, like it always is, 'cause that's where it lives.

"Security, the friendly mask of change

at which we smile, not seeing what smiles behind."

Edward A. Robinson.

"To the Gods, to the Fates, to

the Rulers of men and their destinies."

Someone just played a card known as a "Southern Gentleman."

"It's a sick card, mate."

"No sicker than a *Junker* with student-duel scars on his pan."

"Where are the wars of yesteryear?"

(And the essential foes.)

"Dear dead women, with such hair too,

used to hang and brush their bosoms.

I feel chilly and grown old.
I feel like Tiresias,
[a] fortnight dead, and the waves pick his bones in whispers"
—the old, old words.

Last night—dream of a cold gray beach with sagging fences and
rusty R.R. tracks, muddy waves coming in.

No one is swimming, and no wonder—cold as it is—job for
the "Polar Bear Club," who break the ice and jump in.

"All dope dealers should be executed," says the bloated Newt.

And he is also going to crack down heavy on teen preg-
nancies. And injections of marijuana and sex across the state
line . . .

"What is it in a man's blood that makes him like that?"

Must see Charlie Kincaid about my bleeding gums. Looks like
a chronic low-grade infection:

"Well, Charlie, between you and me we could beat this vile
thing, and send it back into the ooze it oozed out of."

So many terrible scenes with—

forget it, deactivate it, let it go, it is only in your memory now,
remove it.

You have the power to do it.

Write now—

May 15, 1997. Thursday

Just finished *The Last Don*.

I have no real feeling against murder. So many people are just
a permanent pain. So why not?

The first target assigned to "Cross" is this horrible "poet," with liberal, knee-jerk opinions. Awful. Blows his top off with jealousy of his wife, the daughter of the governor of Nevada (very important to the Mob). And stabs her in both eyes, gives hisself a perfunctory stab in the stomach, pleads temporary insanity and walks.

He is Cross's bones. And it couldn't have happened to a lousier creep.

"But then they ask me to kill my uncle Wideman, and I can't."

I can't kill to order, without knowing who I am asked to kill. A man who kills to order degrades himself like a whore who fucks to order.

Old days, when heroin was $28 an ounce and gold the same price.

Not exactly, gold was $35 per ounce for years, until it went gold wild: $300—$400—$500.

Fold sweet etcetera to bed.

So—

How great!

and how out of date.

A time scene

perfectly created

using stolid heavy

characters like

Almayer—

and Lord Jim forever.

Lord of some remote

village up a somber

stream.

And the notorious Captain Seward subsides into a heap of old bones.

And the Steward in the Shadow Line [went] back to Blighty and registered as a heroin addict, died at Prince's Square in Bayswater.

"The look that nigger clerk gives me in Boots's, like I was a nigger—*throws* my heroin at me."

Better stay on in the Orient, where it's cheap and easy, and what is there for me in England? Cold gas heaters waiting for a shilling. Lukewarm bath for two shillings.

Fog and gloom.

Gloom and fog.

I think I stay

where I am—

with my little bottles cheap here—

What's left for me in Tipperary?

May have to leave. Putting aside good emergency [supply] of pills: morphine, heroin, opium—small pills.

Could happen.

"All pernicious foreigners *out!*"

And I leave with what I can take.

Back in England, find out my one contact has died six months ago. Check into anonymous boardinghouse in Prince's Square, Bayswater.

May 16, 1997. Friday

So here we are—back where Bass outlaw breathed his last—last breaths flecked with blood.

"What you doing here, kid? You got some kind of complaint?"

The boy walks over real sheepish and opens the back of a pickup to reveal a hideous swarming of larval creatures, ravenous, with prehensile teeth and claws.

"Well you should know, Doc."
Shall we sit it out here with the guns and ammo we got?
And so why bother, for nothing like that?
We didn't.

EXTRA
Special Edition. May 17, 1927. Saturday

(Look I put down *1927* when I mean *1997*. But I live at 1927 Learn Hard Street and it's a hard bore. So date, address, year, time 4:50 [P.M.])

Reading *Invasion*, by Robin Cook.

Little black disks rain down on a dull town—I mean heavy dull. Any more teenage talk over Banana and marshmallows . . .

Well, the disks appear seamless, but a slit will open, a needle pop out, and a drop injected. Flu for a matter of hours for the young and healthy, death for sufferers from chronic illness (diabetes, arthritis).

Those who recover are transformed for the better. They are stronger, healthier, more confident and concerned with important factors, like rain forest and environment.

So I can't see why Casey and Pitt and Jesse are so concerned to stop this thing. I say give it a boost.

(I haven't heard from John D.C. in some time. Remember he used "sane" for "same," like: "It's all the sane.")

Well, with such madness at touch of a disk, who wants to retain a dead, dreary, crushing weight of sanity, where it's all the sane? What is their motivation? It's, well—inhuman. And thank your little disk for that.

Now here is a streetwise kid:

"Must be a catch in it. When everybody is in—*snap!* The trap closes. And so Homo Sap relieves a protein shortage on Planet X."

But why always take such a negative view? If someone now smiles who never did before, if people get more open in their sex life?

I have yet to see anything but good in the disks. Rain 'em down on Lawrence. It's too much "the sane" here.

It's the slow pressure breaks a man.

So why in the fucking hell, Cook, are you so set against what looks like a real face-lift for Planet Earth?

With a monarch's voice, I call for change—"all is in the not done, the diffidence that faltered."

You think there is something intrinsically magnificent in Homo Sap?

It is time to demonstrate this wondrous excellence in the little time that remains.

A pestilence of night that depopulates the earth?

What will become of the cats? The dogs? Fish in aquarium?

So be careful about—

Way back early days of the cut-up:

"Betraying the least sober soul orders

Releases a great pestilence of night."

Everyday it's all the sane

The same blue heaven, the same lane

tomorrow and tomorrow and

demain—to the last syllable of recorded

time.

"How dull it is to pause, to

    make a rest, to rest unburnished,

    not to shine in use."—Tennyson

May 17 or 18, 1997

And so here is the left-behind *Sneer*.

May 17, 1997

We call this "Day of the Live *and* the Dead."
　　Goodness will open to them, and plenty.
　　But not too much.
　　"The mills of God grind
　　slowly, but they grind
　　exceeding small."

May 23, 1997. Friday

Great day Wednesday, with the ME TOO Band in Kansas City.
　　I love these public appearances, like an injection of sincere reciprocal goodwill.

> *"I'll go right back where
> the bullets fly and
> stay on the cow
> until I die."*

Here I crack up laughing.
　　Trying to come up with a really *new* reading, [that] would really put across who I am and what I am here for:
　　"I have to do this."
　　So we start with the big, ugly American lie.
　　Allen Ginsberg, according to George Will, made his career on the dysfunctions of American Society—that is, he [gnawed] a hole in the Lie. And from that *Howl* came *glasnost*. The *Howl* heard

round the world, from Mexico City to Peking and *glasnost* in Russia, the *Howl* of distorted, suffocating youth.

World War II Country Club:

Face red with drink and anger, he reels up to a dignified old fuck.

"Bovard," he snarls, "I could kill you in ten seconds—five, maybe—like this."

"Get your hands off me!"

They fall in a welter of ice cream, chicken *à la king*.

"I'll kill you, Bovard"—he brandishes a carving knife—"if you don't accept my terms."

The *maitre d'* stands by and wrings his hands.

"Nothing like this. Never before in the club, sir."

Suddenly vicious, he whirls:

"Get out of here! I run a decent place."

May 24, Saturday, 1997.

All governments are built on lies. All organizations are built on lies.

Lies can be harmless—

("This is a miracle drug known as Methadone, that removes the desire for Heroin." Sure, like gin relieves the desire for whiskey. However, was the only way to get the methadone clinics started.)

—or malignant, like the lies that inspire the War Against Drugs, which has turned into a War Against Dissent. A war against truth.

Fix yourself on this:

Bennett, late drug czar:

"We must target the casual user. That people can hold jobs and lead orderly lives gives a bad message. *Very dangerous.*"

To whom, exactly?

In other words: only [subservience] to the Lie is RIGHT and decent.

Truth is very dangerous. Nixon said that Leary [was] "the most dangerous man in America."

Once again: dangerous to whom, exactly, and in what way?

Like Allen Ginsberg: he made a hole in the big, ugly American lie, and in the other lies as well. He was an international icon of truth, openness, *glasnost.*

Consider Bennett's statement about "dangerous users who function in society." It contains [a] basic contradiction: if he targets these dangerous ones, he admits that they already exist, and that he is powerless to contain this menace.

"Well I hope you make it, Kid. May I fall down and be paralyzed if I don't mean it. I know how tough it can get, and if it does get too tough, well just so happens I got it right here in my pocket."

Who are these anti-drug freaks? Where [do] they come from, for chrissakes? Where do they think they are going?

"Marijuana decreases short-term memory, interferes with coordination, causes lung cancer." (And rots the brain and moral values.)

Fact: Cannabis is one of the best anti-nausea drugs, and increases appetite and general well-being. Also stimulates visual centers in the brain. I have gotten so many excellent images from cannabis. It is also the only subtle and effective aphrodisiac in existence. I used no other in my salad days, and "*quelle accouplements!*"—"and what couplings!"—as an admiring French critic exclaimed.

Come here!

Who are you, to whom truth is so dangerous?

What is truth?

Something immediately seen as truth: self-evident spiritual truth.

(Ruled out of consideration by the Scientific Method. It may appear only once. It may not be repeatable.)

We make truth. Nobody else makes it. There is no truth we don't make.

Punch a hole in the Big Lie. Punch a hole for me. Punch a hole for "magic casements opening on the foam of perilous seas in fairy lands forlorn." (Keats)

Allen made holes in the Big Lie, with his poetry and with his presence of self-evident spiritual truth.

Last words: "Two to five months, the doctors said."

Allen said, "I think much less."

Then he said to me:

"I thought I would be terrified, but I am *exhilarated!*"

His last words to me.

I recall talking on the phone with him *before* the deadly diagnosis, and it was there in his voice—remote, weak.

I knew then.

Howl to Mexico City, Peking, *glasnost*—yes, and [there are] those who are pleased by his death.

Get some "Milestones" ready for "bad rubbish."

So it is here or there—in the wall?

Animals in the Wall?

Giraffe and a Kangaroo in the wall.

Like some said about the death of Tim Leary:

"Good riddance to bad rubbish."

Anybody said that is talking about his own demise, the sooner the quicker.

Allen punched a hole in the big lie: a howl that was heard from Mexico to Peking from Rome to Russia. His avenue was truth, openness, *glasnost*.

Leary made another. I talked to both Tim and Allen shortly before death.

Leary, the night of death—he said: "Why not?"

Allen, the day before—

"Truth is dissent, where all power resides in the Big Lie."

So what is the Big Lie, from Hearst's false Armistice Day, and the Finnish War with Russia—(Too cold at the Front, so they all holed up in the Press Club in Helsinki, guzzling vodka, and concocted absurd front-line reports: soldiers quick-froze[n], with their rifles aimed but never fired.)—to the War Against Drugs.

Bennett: "Marijuana research—"

Facts I can testify to, from personal experience and observation: Many of my best effects in writing are due to this beneficent essence: I can see no way out of a literary *cul de sac* . . . a few drags on the green tit, and I can see multiple ways out, and beyond.

So why all this heat on this harmless and beneficial substance?

While Nicotine kills 400,000 a year and Alcohol—oh my Gawd, how many, in stupid assaults and just plain obnoxious behavior . . .

May 25, Monday, 1927
This is Armistice—I mean Memorial Day.

The search for a final answer—the Holy Grail, Philosopher's Stone.

A receding mirage. Any case, who wants a final answer?

I asked a Japanese physicist: "Do you really want to know the secret of the universe?"

He said "Yes."

I thought: "A fraction of that secret would have you climbing the walls."

Me, I only want to know what I need to know, to do what I need to do.

"Just an old Tech Sergeant, me."

The Big Lie—examples:

"Very dangerous."

"Most dangerous man!"

"*We* say what is true and what isn't. The proof? The People believe what we say."

The Big Lie is what we force or persuade enough people to believe.

Fascism never needed a majority, just 10%, plus the military and the police. And how easy to persuade, when a little piece of power is the carrot.

Ho hum—the corruptible planet, and the "un-corruptibles" are the shits of all creation.

The war against drugs is a war against dissent. A move to [a] police state, on *international* extension. It is also a war against Blacks.

So who is at the top of that?

Hard-line Wasps, who say: "*That* son of a bitch," when my name comes up.

"*Je suis un vieux combatant!*"

Recall Jean-Jacques Lebel doing this number at a reading, about 1959–60. It was good.

(What a fool I was in those days.)

So at 83, I finally catch up to myself.

In terms of where I came from, I am just emerging from a stormy adolescence with a modicum of sense.

So to see the world whole?

"You can keep quite comfortable on Codeine."

Where are all the junkies gone? Long time passing?

May 26, Monday, 1997.

I quote from a spy book, *The Secret Is Out:*

"Colonel Alfred Real was one of the most notorious double agents who ever lived. To honorable men and women, there is no one more despised than an agent who betrays his own people for personal gain."

What rubbish! The superior and perceptive man has no people. We leave that to the Niggers, the Jews, the Chinks and the Red Necks.

The Americans are *my* people? Some are. Some English, French, Italians, Germans—not many.

Oh, *all my fans,* of course, are my people—in a very literal sense. Who else buys and reads my books? My fans are my people.

I leave that to the niggers and the Jews. They got people. I don't got no people, except my fans and my characters. They walk off the page. X marks the spot.

Speaking of peoples, my own people—the Wasps, the financiers—(my Uncle Ivy Lee, well known as "Poison Ivy," was publicity man for Rockefeller. Big operator. Never liked me. I *saw* too much.)

Seeing later became my trade; at that time, it was just—

"That boy gives me the creeps."

"It is a walking corpse."

Now a new slant on reading. Song and dance?
   "Ain't it strange, without a doubt.
   Nobody knows you when
   you're down and out.
   Then as soon as you get up
   on your feet again,
   everybody wants to be your
   long-lost friend."
   Marlene Dietrich:
   "Too old, he's too old to cut the mustard any more."

Now here is a poem by Wordsworth, called "Michael." Short and simple [annals] of the poor.
   This old farmer had a son named Michael, and they were building together a stone fence to keep the sheeps in or out. Then Michael went away to London; fell into bad company. He isn't coming back.
   "So many times the old man went down to the fence,
   and never lifted up a single stone."

Do I want to know? I have tried psychoanalysis, yoga, Alexander's posture method, done a seminar with Robert Monroe (the *Journeys out of the Body* man), EST in London, Scientology, Sweat Lodges and a *yuwipi* ceremony.
   Looking for the answer?
   Why? Do you want to know *the secret?*
   Hell, no. Just what I need to know, to do what I can do.
   "All is in the not done. The diffidence that faltered."
   Ezra Pound (Old Crank)
   And here is a cut-up with Ezra:
   "fool of recent narrow sword

Impotent unguarded
usurers squeezing the air"
Pretty cranky. (continued)
"solid the silence of
Black Beatles"
Where is the cavalry, the space ship, the rescue squad?

We have been abandoned here on this planet, ruled by lying bastards of modest brain power. No sense. Not a tiny modicum of good intentions. One lie piled on another. Lying worthless bastards.

Spike Jones and the musical parody. His "Hawaiian War Chant" is a classic.

What do I have to say?

You have been lied to, exploited, cut off from your birthright.

"Sons of shame and sorrow,
will you cheer tomorrow?
Sons of toil and danger,
will you serve a stranger?"

—and bow down to the Alien Grays? (who don't know emotion, we'll help them to know it.)

Can we ever look each other in the face?

I am willing. Are you?

Give me the answer to a question, I tell what the question was.

Nobody but a fool wants to know what the secret of the universe is. Or thinks that he could understand it.

One thing: It is not out there, dead, to be discovered—but out there *alive, to be created.*

Like the Brion Gysin on Mars.

Alive—

Big rock formation on Mars, for Brion Gysin, his big red picture.

"He's the old doctor."

That's the name they give the part he plays:

"Now here comes the Old Doctor."

"Pulling an eighteen-year-old trick like that."

"So you get away with it (shooting junk) for twenty years. You're only kidding yourself."

(Young man with mustache, decent type.)

"It's a bad habit, Burroughs. Get out of it."

State Narcotics Inspector Goldstein—when he learned I was a Harvard graduate, [he] hit me playfully on the chin:

"Look at you, with *everything,* and wind up a *schmecker.*"

"We aren't all shits."

Cop to Huncke:

"Now, you're just a creep."

So many minds I can look into. Sample, feel, experience.

I want to know the *all,* from conception to death. The final *Comedie Humaine.*

"Counsellors and all that shit."

"You crazy or something, walk around alone?"

"It ain't bothering you is it?"

"Pregnant, of course."

Two London working-class blokes passing a troop of Boy Scouts:

"That's where those fiends join in. They're fucking the Boy Scouts."

Billy strayed
  Pre-Perlman writing.
  So.
  "For Ugly Spirit shot Joan because—"

Recent dream? The dream sugar like a sort of custard, unbelievably delicious. In one part of the flat, biting mosquitos and flies. *Bad omen.* Biting flies in a dream are said to be a presage of serious illness. Who lives will see.

May 29, Thursday, 1997.

Life review is not orderly account from conception to death. Rather, fragments—
  (Telephone—my eyeglasses are ready.)
  "You can keep quite comfortable on codeine."
  —from here and there:
  "He looks like a sheep killing dog."
  —Said about me by Politte Elvins, Kells's father, who later went nuts with paresis. [He'd] been treating himself: "Doctors are just mechanics."
  "Take Beano for the measles,
  you pay two dollars down."
  —Old song heard at Los Alamos campfire sing, from Henry Bosworth.
  I hate that son of a bitch, if he still lives anywhere. He called me "a goddamn worthless little pup."
  I hanged him in effigy by the big square fireplace in the Big House. I had used a statue of a Boy Scout, with the message around his neck: "Bozzy Bitch, goddamn him."

(Now he later was fired for fooling with the boys, especially the Marsden family—Bob Marsden was a right bitch in his own right.)

A.J. found out about it:

"Yes," he said, "I know everybody who got up that night."

He had his network of snitches.

"What's the safest place in the U.S., Billy?" he needled me, and Connell says: "Where you are."

(Suppose you are on death row? I guess Fort Knox is about the safest place, offhand—all that gold. Or maybe a vault in Zurich, tended by gnomes.)

It was out by the sawdust pile, caughted fire and been smoldering for years like a mattress.

Recollect in New Orleans Joan set her bed on fire with a cigarette. I was the one woke up. We pour a wastebasket full of water down one hole, and it starts smoking down the other end. Took four metal wastebaskets to quell the fire, and it took $50 to quench the landlady.

Dropped my drink into a wastebasket at the sight of a Glöck double trigger.

If they would—

May 31, 1997. Saturday

"A green thought in a green shade."

"At my back I always hear
Time's wingéd chariot hurrying near."

Took a bath this morning.

Doug and Stephanie of I.O.T. for dinner tonight.

Reading an epidemic book called *Replicator Run,* by Rainer Rey. Pretty good. Symptoms like third-degree burns.

How's about a run of "spontaneous combustions"? They flare up anywhere—or a disease that is spread by the smell, an accelerated rot, from inside out (spread by a tiny red centipede, swarms crawl out of suppurating sores—or the penis crawls away on its own).

That vile salamander Gingrich, Squeeker of the House, is slobbering about a drug-free America by 2000. What a dreary prospect! Of course, this does not include alcohol and tobacco, of which the consumption will soar—and the last state of these United States will be worse than the first. Why is total conformity seen as so desirable?

And how can this drug-free state be achieved?

Simple. A simple operation can remove the drug receptors from the brain. Those who refuse the operation will be deprived of all rights. Any landlord can refuse them housing, any restaurant or bar can refuse service.

What about people in great pain?

"We must make some sacrifices to combat this menace!"

Drug testing, of course. Mandatory for all citizens—refusal to be tested incurs the usual removal of all privileges: no passport, no benefits from Social Security, no medical coverage, no right to buy or own a firearm.

June 2, Monday, 1997.

I wonder if the country will ever wake up to the fact of an international police state under the ever-flimsier pretext of the so-called war against drugs.

Are we going to stand still for this shit?

"Sons of toil and danger,
will you serve a stranger?"

—who, for some reason "we cannot know," needs total conformity of the human hosts.

Why?

For one thing, to cover their parasitic and ill-intentioned presence. And that they must have Homo Sap really broke down to knee-jerk conformity before revealing their actual intentions:

Extermination.

Vot else?

"Sons of shame and sorrow,

will you cheer tomorrow?"

—and enter the slaughterhouse, like good human saps?

Or?

Why not?

Hit them where they are the weakest, and no talk of terms on their terms. Hit now, below the belt.

Cars line up and down Learnard. What's up? What's down? Still inching along a usually empty street. Detour from where? To when and where? And why and who?

Question in hieroglyphs: "reed and water."

Reeds rustled by wind,

reflected in water.

Reeds and water and a shrug.

What is out there?

You cannot know.

Call.

My hand is one of the mysteries.

Enough is enough.

It only takes one.

It only needs one.

As for Humanity, most of them is only good to feed cats.

(Any plague must kill cats and dogs, or a horrible situation will occur: millions of abandoned animals.)

"Nothing is true. Everything is permitted."

Permitted when subject knows that nothing is true. Literally.

"These our actors were all spirits and are melted into air, into thin air."

The only way out is up.

Way up high. With Sky Vodka. More or less.

It was a long time ago, and not at all—as the Catholics like to put it:

"You can compromise until you compromise your point out of any point."

Book *Replicator* [*Run*], by Rainer Rey: "National panic"—since when did a man who is a man Panic?

National Panic?

Everybody inside, with his weapons to protect hisself and his loved ones.

Outside:

"*Sauve qui peut.*"

Every man for himself.

"*Chacun pour soi.*"

SOS. SOS. SOS.

May Day. Aid Me. Aid me.

SOS.

So many old, inept memories clinging like dust and cat hairs.

Stand up—

June 4, 1997. Wednesday

Funny thing I said once—Dave Wollman and me was walking up the twisting, empty Tangier street at 1:00 P.M., and Dave said:

"I think we have company."

And indeed, three ratty-looking Arabics were trailing behind us.

So I reared back and snapped:

"They'll quail before a good woman's gaze!"

I can see the dusty street, the Arabs are just shadows—"incapable of initiating action, helpless and brutal, but infinitely"—from years of living in the streets—"capable of taking advantage of any weakness in another."

(Fitzgerald, "A Short Trip Home.")

They didn't get the green light. We walked on to our siestas, unmolested.

"*Je suis un vieux combatant.*"

—Jean-Jacques Lebel in a reading, *circa* 1959, Paris. Free of the impregnable ego of the French. It was a great reading.

I saw him frequently. In Bourges he introduced me to Jacques Lang, the Minister of Culture. (Gotta drop some names to season my "memoires," or "grimoires," as the case may be.)

Just reminder to: "call me Eddie."

I won't forget Eddie:

"Some people puke from being junk sick."

I never did before, but after fifteen years of methadone??

Reed and water what?

Who lives will see.

"*J'aime ces types vicieux, qu'ici montrent la bite.*"

"I like the vicious types who show the cock here"

—anonymous, outside pissoir in Paris.

"Is it not fine to dance and sing while the bells of death do ring, to turn on the toe and sing hey nonny no."

London [in the] time of plague.

Yes, I love life in all its variety, but at last the bell ringeth to eventide.

How I hate those who are dedicated to producing conformity. For what purpose? Not well-intentioned, from point of view of Homo all-too-Sap. *Hein?*

Imagine the barren banality of a drug-free America. No dope fiends, just good, clean-living, decent Americans, from sea to shining sea. The entire area of dissent has been exorcised, like a boil. No dissent anywhere. No slums. No areas of vague under-cover operations. No nothing.

There in the pitiless noon streets. No letters. One session in session room, and you believe it.

How good will it be
to have total conformity?
What will be left of singularity?
and personality?
and you and me?
eccentricity,
anything that separates you from Me—
waiting to absorb us all.
Not sure where we is going.
Feed the possums on paté.
"You can keep quite comfortable on paté."

June 6, Clom Friday, 1997.

(you won't be un-disappointed)

I wonder about [the] future of the novel, or any writing.

Where is it going, or where can it go? After Conrad, Rimbaud, Genet, Beckett, St.-John Perse, Kafka, James Joyce—

Paul Bowles, Jane Bowles—these two in a special category of doing one thing very well. With Paul a sinister darkness, like underdeveloped film.

With Jane? How do her characters move about, and what can motivate them. But really it's just too special to formulate.

What is left to say?

Oh, I forgot Graham Greene. *The Power and the Glory.*

And Hemingway?

Maybe there is just so much "juice," as Hemingway calls it—and not quite enough to get him in with the select: Joyce [et al.].

"Not quite enough, Papa. You kill yourself from vanity, self-inflation, and when the balloon is ruptured—"

He knew he was finished:

"It just doesn't come anymore."

He just wasn't there anymore.

Back to writing—"*revenons a ces moutons.*"

Maybe there just isn't any more to say, on the basic truth level. Conrad said a lot of it in *Under Western Eyes* and *Lord Jim*—

And Genet, on the Spanish coast—I can feel his hunger, going down by the docks where the fishermen would throw him a fish maybe, which he cooked over a brush fire and ate without salt.

Why go on?

"The tram made a wide U-turn and stopped. It was the end of the line."

Paul Bowles, end of *The Sheltering Sky.*

Sky. Sky.

I can't even write the word "sky."

I guess I feel—

Why go on?

June 6, 1997 (continued)

"The snow was general all over Ireland . . . like the descent of their last end, on all the living and the dead."

(Get *Dubliners* and quote it right.)

"I know the trick," the old terrorist cackles.

Under Western Eyes.

Ginger touches me with her old paw when she wants something. She just touched me, and I let her out.

"Sad as the death of monkeys." *Anabasis.*

Remember the death of the monkey in *Toby Tyler and the Circus.*

Bill Willis's old Fatima—he would admonish her gently for spilling something:

"Uncontrolled slut!"

She would come to me for comfort. Old and frail, like Ginger.

That was in Marrakech.

You can keep quite comfortable in Marrakech.

Bits of film. John Hopkins's parrot. His Fatima, with gold teeth, who talked to herself all the time—loud.

"Am I boring you?"

"Excruciatingly."

See what I mean about the future of writing.

Now I'm a writer myself, if you ask me—a humble practitioner of the scrivener's trade. The Shakespeare Squadron in the war years.

[Unstrung] heroes. Awfully depressing, all that.

"You reckon ill
who leave me out

when me you fly,
I am the wings."
"The old, old words."
The Nigger of the Narcissus.
1900: What safety, stability, a different light. Gone forever now.
The earth has been violated by the atom bomb. No longer
innocent. It was the Apple, and the Pentagon slobbed it down,
boiling blood drooling from their smacking lips:
"Just let me sample some more of that."
"Don't bother me with the war. It's such a bloody bore."
(You're getting a bit vague, old thing. Why not tuck it in for
now?)

"Evil."
What the CIA–Narc. are doing is evil.
No, not just "doing our job"—not at all. Evil. And completely
ill-intentioned, so far as any human potentials are involved.
"Sons of toil and danger—
serve a stranger."
Who is this stranger?
Make self in fingers say:
[automatic writing scribble]
Byrd. Admiral Byrd in the penny-ante South Arctic—down
there, it's the anti-Arctic—I can see leopard seals flipping across
ice floes—and, of course, the inexorable penguins.
This settled—where am I?
I should know?
And if I don't know, I will be the first not to know it.
Now what could be fairer'n that?
And don't take me for dumber than I don't look.
Come closer.

Unsee what you cannot not see.
It is easy when they get the feel of it.
Enough.

A Left Bank movement—*Les Silents,* the Silent Ones, who disdained to reveal themselves, related to Ctulhu and the unclean Old Ones, stewing in their evil for millions of years, stewing it yet more evil all the time.

June 7, 1997. Saturday

"Not much to say," as David Budd said, when I told him old man Wallenda, 73, in Puerto Rico, went out on the wire in a gusty wind.

I saw the TV and could see in his face the moment he knew he wasn't going to make it and fell a hundred feet onto concrete (the wire was strung between two church spires). No net.

"Not much to say!"

Too proud to scream. That would have had a *terrible* effect on the audience.

"His face contorted out of all human resemblance in a scream that shattered wine glasses on discreet tables as he splatters blood over the Press."

Least he could do.

"Little leaves, we too are drifting"

—in hermetic Lesbian bell jars.

"Some day it will be autumn."

Now here is the whole tamale:

"For we had learned from many an autumn
the way in which a leaf can go
lightly, lightly, almost gay,

taking the unreturning way
to mix with winter and the snow . . .
Little leaves, we too are drifting."

"Someday it will be autumn"
—from a Lesbian bell jar, in 1920s–30s, San Francisco.

Drifting—like jellyfish trailing paralyzing tentacles of slow stasis and death, as a hermetic bell jar closes over your head, like the hood over the about-to-be-hanged man's face, to cover "a horrible grimace." (It rhymes.)

Who would like to be in his place, sharing the "horrible grimace"—the *last* "horrible grimace."

At this point I resigned from the Game.

It was a definitive decision, based on what material I had—had—has—have access to, at this time.

June 9, 1997. Monday

What is important?

When was the last time?

I really don't know how to cool the whole "Dream Machine" flurry.

Let it cool down, I say.

Here [is] James, Tom is here. Sort of good acoustics.

I like it *here, now.*

June 10, 1997. Tuesday

Reading *Demons, Etc.* by Felicitas D. Goodman (any relation to Lord Goodman I had the pleasure to know? Head of the Arts Council?)

The Syndrome of Demonic Possession is [as] clearly delineated as any illness. Cases over time, 1800 to present. Germany, Yucatán. It's the same. Subject gives out, or exudes, a terrible stench. Subject screams at the sight or touch of sacred objects—like holy water, crucifix, or the presence of a priest.

"Larry, masturbating hypocrite: take your sheets down to the laundry and wash 'em out yourself . . . Father, *Padre, Vater, Pere*—you and your black robes—you think you can hide under robes, hide your stiff prick?"

They love to embarrass men of the cloth. Why?

Why this fear of holy objects? What is going on here?

Why does the Church oppose research into its own influence and power?

Why so quick to deny exorcism permission?

I think possession is almost universal.

Another way to say [it]:

"Include me out of your 'we'."

—we are all in a prison colony.

I asked the Oracle about who A.J. Connell was, and the answer came back:

"He was a very minor prison official."

So Los Alamos Ranch School was, of course, a prison and indoctrination course.

A.J. asked Mr. Hitchcock if any of these boys realized what they were getting.

"Have you met the Skipper yet?"

And scene with Skipper in Los Alamos front room.

The calm, ironic Skipper—very much Girodias.

Exorcism seems so inadequate:

"Unclean spirits, get out of this creature of God, I command you."

And the "creature of God" is probably a sorry specimen like Holden Caulfield, in *The Catcher in the Rye*.

(Well may he run from fame.)

"What you command, Padre, is a shithouse."

"In the name of the Father and Jesus and the Holy Ghost, I command you to leave the body and soul of William Seward Burroughs II."

June 13, 1997. Friday

Ref: Applicants for God's position.

We got a simple cure. Applicant is stationed in a mid-sized city—sixty thousand, say.

"Now here we are. Shall we take a little tour of *your domain?* Let's start with Mid-Town Memorial Hospital—"

(groans from cancer ward, from maternity and trauma)—

"*You* are responsible for every groan, every scream. You have to *feel* everything, every murder, suicide, depression, psychosis, *all, all, all.*"

Now, most applicants don't make [it] twelve hours.

And those that do? How do they do it?

Mostly by turning off the feel line, as many doctors and nurses do—[they are] Disqualified.

Some hang in for the positive feel, there's nothing like it.

Look at a painting by Pissarro. A road, a cottage, a woman with basket. You are *there.* The pain doesn't touch you here, or by the stream at Giverny.

It isn't all hate and fear and pain, and grating falseness—

—like Mary McCarthy's "Young Man," in hospital next room to a cancer case. He is woked up one night by tasty screams.

"The cancer patient at last!" he ejaculates.

"Cast a cold eye on life

Cast a cold eye on Death

Horseman pass by,"

He sings out lustily.

Next day he says to the nurse:

"I heard screams last night. Was that the *cancer patient?*"

"Uh, uh no. Maternity most likely. You'll never hear a sound out of Mrs. Miller."

"Ohhh."

His lustiness leaks out.

"Only case I ever saw where a healthy young man, in for minor surgery, perfectly sound heart, just stopped on the operating table for no reason, just stopped."

It had no reason to continue.

This is a horrible animal.

—So what keeps an applicant in there?

Those moments: *The Thief's Journal,* J. Joyce, Beckett. The *potentials.*

So now look at the rejects—

So now look at the faces of Hell: faces of great evil, hatred and *despair.* Cut off from the *light.*

It's a utility. Can be cut off.

Why? Hummm.

One God? He urpa out the Lucifer family.

Back to the Rejects: atheist, "scientific [secular] humanist"— (what a miserable creature it must be).

So the Rejects are those who just don't make it as anything—so they are glad of the chance to become simple, down-to-earth fucking Demons. That usually means they have a special area of influence.

June 14, 1997. Saturday

Certainly the RA's (Rejected Applicants) form the basic cadre of possessing demons—they flunked out, and now they of course hate the point of their failure.

They could not love. Sounds sappy, but love is a very definite force, like electricity.

They lost it, never had it?

I wonder.

They didn't get grace. Couldn't get grace.

(The examples: Walter Ramsay and the Young Man, both I cited as far from grace as a man can get.)

"What is it in a man's blood makes him like that?"

—Hemingway.

"*Quién es?*"

The Wishing Machine, made correctly with copper plates—highest success rate on Japanese beetles, corn borers, caterpillars. Is it such a jump to heartworms?

We could found, right here, the *Miracle Heart Worm Clinic*.

Dogs and cats come in emaciated, lifeless. They frisk out of the clinic.

"First things first," I snapped.

Gray fever, *old* dead [hand], arthritis-withered.

I don't care.

Grace for me came in the form of a cat, Ruski, and then other cats—all cats and lemurs and weasels. Etcetera.

Now here is a G.A. [God Applicant] can't take the pain of burn victims, cancer—

So he takes it in his face.

The hideous grimaces of the Demon: a hideous parody of pain.

Why pain? Fear? Death? Hate? War?

No war, no friction. No friction, no life.

It's just as simple as that:

"We like friction, and we hate each other."

Just as simple as that, isn't it.

Look, it's too tiresome—good guys and bad guys, from here to eternity.

As Sri Aurobindo said (it was the last thing he said, from a ten-year trance):

"It is all over."

All animals are a part of you. Why so many parts rejected, demonized, dreaded, exterminated?

Like the Thylacine in Tasmania, the only marsupial wolf, wiped out by the *bestial* settlers—posing with dead Thylacines they have killed personally.

Seems a Thylacine killed a sheep, and a bounty followed, and the last Thylacine died in 1936 in a Tasmanian zoo. Sightings here and there, nothing definite.

The last Thylacine, crippled by a hunter's bullet, limps away to extinction.

I *hate* the settlers, of course, they don't even think that their own position is equally tenuous.

They don't think—slurping down on—

June 15, 1997. Sunday

"Gloomy Sunday."

The suicide song, suppressed everywhere, singers jailed for singing it, still it emerges through subway grates and manholes with the steam . . . an old bum with frayed-stringed homemade violin quavers it out: "Gloomy Sunday."

And I think it should be suppressed—it's terrible schmaltz, at its most false and tawdry.

Does Christ never get tired of bleeding? He does—but the show must go on.

Where?

Consider bright green folk:

"My color doesn't mean anything."

Just stops traffic, is all.

Black people is different from dappled whitish folk. The look out the eyes is different. I know—walking up this dark street and the look out my eyes different, and met a black woman who looked at me and said:

"Hello, Mr. Faustus."

Well he don't have the papers on me.

So don't take me for dumber than I look. None so blind as he who will not look.

That dreariest of roles, "the scientific [secular] humanists"—the *Skeptical Inquirer*. Three times I sent their subscription back—anybody doesn't believe in ESP hasn't kept his eyes open.

"Do you want the eyes removed before he leaves the hospital?"

"Oh, yes of course, and *circumcised* too."

Do I need your prejudicial and regurgitated and re-this-and-that—to make up my mind on any subject?

Three times, and they kept coming:

"You can't be serious, an intelligent enlightened man."

What's his name—[Carl Sagan] has wroted a fat book to combat the wave of irrational (and long suppressed) influences that threaten to engulf us all in a wave of superstition and proliferating cults, all dedicated to salvation in some imaginary Heaven of their own concocting.

"When evening is nigh"
(the bouncing sing-along ball)
"I hurry to my blue heaven."

June 17, 1997. Tuesday

Must send a check to the [Duke University] Primate Center for the lemurs, how I love them!

Yes, I do love animals, to the detriment of human animals—who can, in many cases, unfortunately, TALK. Loud and long, and to very little purpose.

Well, good ones and bad ones.

"That's what you get for trying."

"Fifteen men on the dead man's chests—"
(yeah, he always traveled with two chests, often three)
"Yo Ho HO and a bottle of rum.
Drink and the Devil had done for the rest.
Yo ho ho and a bottle of rum."

"It was down in LeHigh Valley,
me and my brother Lu.
We was looking for a whorehouse
and a good one too."
"Go to the House of David

and watch the girls eat shit—
makes a man feel good all over."
"See me fuckee sister?"
"Oh you big bad man."
"Taking your love on the easy plan,
here and there and where you can."
"Brother can't you spare a dime."
"Some day it will be autumn."
"Who were [you] when the plane was called?"
"Do you think it was some nurse you were talking to in that
hospital?"
"You can keep quite comfortable on Codeine."
"I may be old but I'm still desirable."

Allen Ginsberg:
   The Beat movement was more a socio-political movement than
a literary one.
   (What a crippled sentence. It should crawl away and die.)
   Allen's influence was not a special American genius, as George
Will attempts to contain it, but [the] worldwide influence of a
man speaking the truth, to the best of his vision.
   When Allen first talked to me about Blake and—I thought,
"oh my God another *mental*." But with his innate humor and
common sense, he rode out the cosmic currents, and achieved
a remarkable fusion of Buddhism, of which he was a devoted
follower—
   "[In] any case you can see we are completely booked up."
   So he proceeded on his written way, unperturbed, calm, un-
assuming.
   Informed of a two- to four-month life expectancy, he said:
"I think much less."

The message from his body was clear. He died the next day.

Instead of denial, he looked and saw the truth—

"I thought I would be terrified but I am actually *exhilarated*."

This reaction to Death—well, they say that cats purr at the approach of death.

I think of Spooner. What a perfect cat—that is exactly what he was designed to be, [and] he was.

One of my dedicated Literary Enemies, Anatole Broyard, reports a similar exhilaration. When prostate cancer, of which his father had died, left little time he wrote an article: "Intoxicated by My Illness." He was high on the approach of death. Nothing wrong with that.

Allen's influence was worldwide . . . he was deposed as Queen of the May in Prague and asked to leave:

"We do not like your new sexual theories, Mr. Ginsberg. You will be driven to the airport."

But by and large, he was well seen by the authorities. [He] talked with [Richard] Helms and the professor turned intelligence agent [James Jesus Angleton]. [They] told Allen how they had whisked Ezra Pound off to St. Elizabeth's Hospital before the FBI [could take] him into custody to stand trial for capital treason. (The name Phillip Angel?)

[Hoover] had all this discrediting dope on—"I have a dream," he said—OK, Martin Luther King. It all comes flooding back.

"Memories of nursing school. But it has to be done. So let's go."

You see before you the Grand Old Man of Letters—taking a bow.

(Angleton, then head of the CIA. Said maybe he should have been a poet instead of a spy. Safe-behind-the-lines spy, eh Phillip? Know the angles don't you? *Are* the angles.)

So there is little that remains.

Lowell Wadman, a Federal Prosecutor in NYC.

"Addicts," he said, "you speak to them harshly—'look, your lip is trembling.'"

This was a fishing trip, Montana, out at Missoula.

"Expensive habit. Cost $40 a week, less usually, $20 per week."

In those days $20 was a good week's salary. Big Nichols' breakfast, two eggs, hash browns, three bacon strips, toast, coffee was then 35 cents. Now $3.50, plus $2.00 tip.

So a habit was a habit in those good old days, when heroin was $28 an ounce. Too much of a good thing can become a very, very bad thing.

Last night more dreams of water and fishing and other matters. I cannot recall at this moment.

I hear José's voice so loud now and clear, but what does it say?

I hear it now. And what does it say?

José, what do you say?

Is talking in Spanish:

"*Huéspede.*"

In Ecuador.

"*No es de—*"

many long years ago
the old old gray mare
she ain't what she used to be
many long years ago.

Yagé mucho da—
Many long years ago

It little profits that an idle king— How dull it is to pause, to make a rest . . . not to not to shine in use.

June 20, 1997. Friday

The actor is good in nasty, pimping part, with his ragged mustache. Good nasty hands to beat a whore up.

June 21, 1997. Saturday

The actor comes here tonight.

I find it difficult to remember my dreams—but a few are outstanding: a pool I had dug that was 30 feet deep. It was in the middle of a bare muddy lot. Swimming the Mississippi with José.

Now here is the prize: a slender boy, inhumanly beautifully in the front room. He was wearing a yellow hat with a red brim so I could see only the perfect outline of his face. Yellow jacket and pants like yellow silk, sandals in leather with gold trim. He said nothing.

I went down in the basement and there he is again. Just standing there. No words. No gestures, but . . .

"Would you like to be me? *Eh, pués?*" ("And then?")

The dream I have waited for so long?

Something of the circus about him. An actor. Oriental. *Un peu.* Too perfect to be sexually attractive. Sex was out of the question. We never touched.

Sudden flash! He is Russian or Tartar. Now I see a short curved sword at his side, and a small pistol, of a design unknown to me. One weapon on one side, one on the other. Of course. Always. The

pistol on the right side of thick red silk sash, the sword on the left.
Or maybe the whole military garb is an illusion. What isn't? But I
remember him from the dream about Door Dogs, a long time ago.

June 22, 1997. Sunday

A veteran German refugee—(I married Ilse Herzfeld Klapper to
get her into the USA, so I know the genre)—so this experienced
refugee said to me:

"When someone tells me they are *broke*, I say: 'Have you no
pride?'"

"Pride is a luxury I can no longer afford."

"That happened long ago, *mon semblable, mon frère.*"

"But what have I to give you?"

Lifts his hands sadly and turns them out:

"Monkey bones, of Eddie and Bill?"

There was a time—

"Time was, Time is, Times Past."

"You see Mrs. Norton, that's just what *we* are here for: to give
reassurance and total safety to people like you and your husband."

"We will never leave your side," said the thin, snide agent in a
trench coat and felt hat.

"You just feel danger and you look up—there we will be, portentous as comets."

"Ah yes to be sure—but we are also discreet."

Look at Heaven and Hell for a moment as a feud between crime
families. Think of the murders, and the tortures [the] Good Don
must have been through over a million years—but before that,
the whole Zoo Project—he is now trying to weasel out from
under, and leave US with the check.

What is going on with USA. Top officials is *so rotten*, a man can't believe it. Such a complete sell-out.

9:45 A.M. an upsetting revelation:

I seem to have lost the capacity for fear—psychic fear.

The body fear is still there—or is body fear always behind psychic fear?

June 24, 1997. Tuesday

Reading a novel set in Los Alamos, in the mad days of the Manhattan Project.

Here we are at a typical party, square dance, cowboy music, but the dancers are all scientists. Very special ones too.

I note the thing lacking in this travesty of a Square Dance Rustic scene, that would always be there in the "real world": danger—the potential for violence, always *there* but not *here*. Scientists do not ram broken glasses into an offending face. They do not kick a quarters boy in the crotch. So it's all out of joint, a masquerade.

As "Oppie" puts it:

"We are all ghosts. We don't exist. Security, you know."

Must have been a most unreal scene—Los Alamos I mean.

I remember A.J. [Connell] telling me he had asked Hitchcock, the Latin teacher (only teacher at the Hill made any sense):

"I wonder if the boys know what they are getting here?"

I thought: "good food, good health, and—?"

It seems we were the *selected*—to do what, I don't know.

When I asked the [Oracle]:

"Who was A.J. Connell?"

Answer:

"He was a very minor prison official. His job just to keep the boys in line."

What line?

Beware of whores who say: "I don't want money."

The hell they don't. What they mean is they want more money, much more.

"What you think I am, a whore?"

So Connell meant something when he said: "Your little bean is so limited."

[As] Mary Cooke said: "But, Burroughs, you're so *dumb*. Did you think it was some *nurse* you were talking to in that hospital?"

"Yeah, Burroughs," A.J. said, "you just are not picking up."

He had a point.

June 25, 1997. Wednesday

The Lords, from an old magazine, flaking away in little puff of russet smoke.

The Lords—thousands of years of encrusted evil in the ancient faces, like amber, [vile] as [these] tiny deadly scorpions and centipedes encrusted in their faces. EVIL. They were unbelievably evil, cut off in this remote pocket of space-time. Where Evil has attained a final refinement.

"Strangers." The Lord breathes out, hungrily. "Strangers."

June 28, 1997. Saturday

Am I not mellowed—aged in cats and roses, and fish ponds with multicolored goldfish.

"To open an account, press five."

"You will be surprised at how you will be rewarded."

(Brion's spoof on Renaissance Patrons—rewarded with prison.)

Reminds me of Johnson's magnificent letter to Lord Chesterfield:

"Some five years ago, when I first asked your help on this project (a dictionary), I had already exhausted the means to please that a retiring and uncourtly scholar can possess, and no man likes to have his all rejected. Is not a patron, my lord, one who watches with indifference a man struggling in the water, and when he has reached shore, encumbers him with help? Your help, had it been early, I would have deeply appreciated. But it has been delayed until I am solitary and cannot share it, until I am known and do not need it."

(This is from memory and needs reference to original.)

Johnson said of Lord Chesterfield's letters to his son:

"They teach the manners of a dancing master, and the morals of a whore."

Leads me to an old project—favorite passages.

Interview in *Under Western Eyes* between Councillor Mikulin and (one of those Russian names).

Talk between Marlowe and the French Naval Officer in *Lord Jim*.

Start with Trimalchio's Feast in Petronius.

The Unfortunate Traveler.

Fury by Kuttner.

The Siren Web and the Happy Cloak—

Roderick Random, the doctor, drunk out of his mind, lopping off limbs at a great rate.

The shorts, like: "If your trick no work you better run."

The fact that something is quoted from someone else or somewhere [else] gives it a magical gloss, the portentous found-object.

If [it] can be a found, a woodcut of Baudelaire on hash.

"Portentous as a comet."
J'aime ces types vicieux
qu'ici montrent la bite"
"Simon, *aime tu le bruit*
de pas sur les feuilles mortes?"
"Is it not fine to dance
and sing, while the bells
of Death do ring?"
"Oh to be in England, now
that April is there."
April Ashley, a sex-change. Last saw her, it, at the Chelsea Arts
Club. (Great breakfasts and lunches.)

An anonymous queen I met in the Bounty Bar, Mexico, D.F.:
"I may be old, but I'm still desirable."
"Don't take me for dumber than I look."

The bank robber in Canada with the sweetest voice any bank
teller ever heard:
"Everybody, please put your hands up high."

You better believe it. He said:
"When I kill someone I get a terrible gloating feeling."

And the one in Chicago, and there would be pictures too—
The Chicago Fiend, a little skinny man with superhuman
strength, could pick up a two-hundred-pound detective like he
weighted a feather.

"Oh yes," he said, "you will hang me, but I won't be there."
News photo of Fiend, carried out of cell in a chair:
"He stunned himself with yoga."

"I'll wake the bastard up," says the fat guard, his eyes sizzling
like hot gray grease. He shoves his cigarette out on his arm. No
reaction. He does it again. No reaction.

"Shit, we'll get a chair."
It was done.

"I swear he was already forty-eight hours dead when they hanged him," the doctor said.

"I got no enemies. I turn 'em all into friends, one way or another."

"You can keep quite comfortable on Codeine"

"And never lifted up a single stone."

What is the answer? What is the question?

"The Skipper answered never a word, a frozen corpse was he."

June 29, 1997. Gloomy Sunday

I reflect on the agent lingo, "dropping the double," where every word carries a double—or more—*meanings*.

"A *certain* very small *fish* found only in *inaccessible* mountain *streams*, highly prized by the Japanese as a *very expensive* delicacy?"

"It is amazing the price of *genuine* Ruski caviar, from the very *special* sturgeons, only the *best* Beluga."

Well, let's get on with my *special* quotes from *very* special *people*.

"That's a good one. *Special people*. You old fraud."

Speak of old frauds, Hemingway takes precedence—

The two most atrocious conceits in the English tongue:

"Each little pimple had a tear in it

To wail the fault its rising did commit."

Dryden, "On Lord Hastings' Small Pox"—in this corner.

"The hole in his forehead where the bullet went in was the size of a pencil at the unsharpened end. The hole in the back of his head where the bullet went out was big enough to put your fist in [it], if it was a small fist, and you wanted to put it in there."

Papa Hemingway—in this corner.

"And of course, you know, too late. The knife was already buried to the hilt in his chest."

The Secret Agent, Conrad, set in London.

We go now to:

"Do I?"

"Yes."

Isn't it *not* fine to dance and sing while the bells of death *don't* ring—ring and turn on the toes and shouting out: "Hey nonny no's."

"So what's wrong with that pattern?"

So what's wrong with a sieve to hold water, if that is what the sieve is designed to do?

Well—

So let's just slob it under the rug with the other not-to-be-talked-about. It's easier that way.

For whom is it easier?

Or for whom and what is [it] being made easier, or less so?

June 30, 1997. Monday

Yes, it was a Monday, 1882 when Bob Ford gunned down "Mr. Howard," also known as Jesse James, and laid Jesse James in his grave.

"The dirty little coward who shot Mr. Howard
and laid Jesse James in his grave."

Hardly warm before the Youngers, the others break through—so many—

It was a Monday yesterday. June 30, 1997. It is now a Tuesday.

A call from the Charles Henri [Ford] people at this point. So he took some good photos at the Fair in Paris. ([The] one they are using, in front of a fortune-telling booth.)

He had a flat in the Isle St.-Louis, always a small piece of the best, and the Dakota in NYC, where James and I had a rather disagreeable dinner, and Fred Sparks arrived—and after dinner, on way back home, I likened him to [the] evil old transfer artist in *If I Were You,* by Julien Green:

"My god, what a face! What a filthy face. Marked by age, extreme experience and wickedness."

Well, he looked always indecently young, like he made the Devil's Bargain. (Methinks the Devil got the worst of it.)

Henri was [in] the old *Zero* mob, with Paul and Jane, Carson McCullers, and a goodly crowd was there. He was an individual.

Remember chili con carne at Isle St.-Louis in Paris. Good. The chicken and rice at the Dakota (no cocktails) was atrocious.

Now here is the Old Man of twisters and floods, giving orders to his assassins—through roses, with a cat on his shoulder. Seasoned, but not mellowed, in roses and cats.

The General rings his bell. Guards rush in.

"There's a cat in here!"

"But sir—"

"Don't argue. I heard it mewl."

A search of the commander's bedroom reveals no cat or other intruder, but as soon as the guards have left—*Meeow meeoww.*

And what slot is there for a crazy general?

Man was put on this planet to hybrid with other animals, and reptiles and birds and fish (insects?). Instead, he put his unsightly likeness above all other creatures, so cutting himself off from any infusion of energy and purpose. Weltering in idiotic self—self glorification—to wallow for all eternity in idiot self-worship.

"I no ape. Me man!"

Beats his chest and glares about.

According to Emily Post:

"In a very smart London club, one keeps one's hat on and glares about."

—"Don't looka me!"

—"Who you fucking staring at?"

Something is *wrong*.

"Sorry sir, got the wrong reel."

"You sure have got the wrong reel."

From *The Wild Party:*

"I [don't] like you
and I don't know you
and now by God I'm going
to show you."

July 4, 1997. Friday

For the Glorious Fourth and the atom bomb on Hiroshima.

"We are become [Death], destroyer of worlds," Oppenheimer said.

But was it the 5th or the 6th of July, when the glorious Manhattan Project came to a spectacular?

"Thank God it wasn't a dud."

—Oppenheimer, known as "Oppie" to his friends.

What God [are] you thanking for Hiroshima and Nagasaki, Oppenheimer?

Let it be forgotten, as something that happened light years away, slowly dispersing like morning mist.

"These our actors, as I foretold [you], were all spirits and are melted into air, [into] thin air."

"The great globe itself, and all which it inhabit . . . leaves not a rack behind."

(Get the whole fucking quote right—will you? You could leave things in a state of half-dispersal.)

Who, I ask, can belittle the Immortal Bard?

Bacon wroted it all with his left hand?—Improbability hath wroughted his master work.

Screen flickers back over the Baron Franz von Blomberg, the cheap Irish hustler got a senile old bag claimed to be the daughter of a von Blomberg to "adopt him." Rarely have I seen such naked, pure opportunism in human form as Franz, Baron Blomberg. His card [read]: "Advisor to Royal Families"—and he could always dredge one up.

Just thinking of the horrible people I have known—an inoculation, really.

"*That one* won't land here again."

"Go find a live one!"

"Don't want virus scum in here."

"Steaming off you like heat waves off manure."

Turn it off. It is going nowhere.

Please, help here, help, help.

Help! S.O.S.

Here is the ultimate horror dead end.

I forget: *Sauve qui peut!*

Every man for himself.

Chacun pour soi.

Los Alamos:

"Far away on the mesa's crest

Here's the life that all of us love the best.
Summer days when the balsam breezes blow"
(from the cauldrons of hell)
"Winter days when we skim on the ice and snow."
(A frozen planet where no life as the earth people know it can survive.)
What is survival—survivability? Look straight ahead with everything YOU got. And cut loose with what you and no one else has.
(I am now talking to, say, maybe one in a billion. Oh well, let's not get too elitist—say one in a million? 'Course, we are dealing here in some heavily damaged material. But better to err on the side of clarity than rote bureaucracy? *Hein?*)

You know a real friend?
Someone you *know* will look after *your* cat after *you* are gone.

Remember in *Believe It or Not:* A resident of Paris had this cat. The resident died. The cat could not be lured from the Master's headstone, and died there. To me, one of the most heartrending stories of my knowing.

July 5, 1997. Saturday
Article in *Blade* about "the greatest knife thrower of all time."
I have thrown knives since Los Alamos, when I used to throw a short bayonet into oak fenceposts. Held by the point, it flips over once, then one inch into oak—it *quivers.*
At Los Alamos, Hank Wardwell—stupid little creep, like most of the Los Alamos boys—thought he was stronger, there-

fore he could throw the bloody knife *deeper*. When he found out he couldn't, he looked disgruntled, like he had been basically betrayed.

(I have been impressed by the awesome power of a thrown knife. The strength of the thrower is irrelevant, and often disruptive.)

Another test case: ask *strong* man to take this knife and, using all his strength, to thrust it into target. Knife drops out of wood.

How long to learn. A knife is not pushed into target. Knife is *thrown into* target.

How well could this work with a fist? See your fist as a ball of lead covered with leather, on the end of a flexible, corded, relaxed rope.

Not quite. Something more is needed. Power of the blow gun? Not quite. Getting close. But a thrown rock is not so close. But the spear is?

Yes. I can see the thrower, arms loose as ropes, the fist of a heavy cartilage like the abrasive skin of a shark.

How I miss the old Agent days of total fear and alertness—

Gone now. Gone slack, and for me little remains, far on the windy plains of Troy.

Where the hounds of Spring are on Winter's traces
and mother of—
on windy Troy.

Fills the great empty places where no thing is—
Samadhi.
Total Silence.
Total.
Not peace, because peace can only exist with war.

July 6, 1997. Sunday

Answered a letter from Dave Wollman ref. death of Allen Ginsberg. My "Roses Picture."

The Old Man gives his assassins orders through the roses, with a purring cat on his shoulder.

Flash—back to Tangier. A dark street with Dave and the Portuguese *maricón*—(forget his name. He died in Madrid. O.D., I think. He had it coming. We all do.).

"Put another notch in my gun, Mike."

So Mexico, D.F., the cheapest kick.

My God! Cheap! Cheap American!

Suppose.

Dream—strong opposition. James had—what was it, then he had done it. Done what?

Back to the campus of Chicago U. I was making dangerous inquires at the Egyptology Department. That was back in the late [1930s]. Dangerous for what, or whom? Way back there, and me with no training. I still heard a frantic voice saying:

"You don't *belong* here!"

As if the Herr Professor screams out:

"You filthy thing stinking out my office, I'll have the couch burned."

And the Priest screams through the confessional slot:

"You filthy abomination, if I had my way I'd tear your balls off."

July 8, 1997. Tuesday

The doctor snarls:

"I can hardly endure the vile stench of your filthy ass cancer. Nurse! Bring me a mask, and soak in Chanel [No.] 5."

Good shooting yesterday at Fred's. I can't miss with my .45 long Colt S&W Target model. But the Colt Python has broke itself down after six shots. I am calling McColl. Back to the Colt factory! It's their top gun! Give me one that works, or give me my $800 back. Would I had spent it on an old Sheffield tip-up 5-barrel .45 Colt! Or the S&W Mountain gun, in .45 long Colt.

Now that fucking python done *squeezed* 800 Georges outa me, and all it is is a good-looking paperweight. Got a nice finish to it.

Gathering my brows like
a gathering storm
and nursing my wrath
to keep it warm.

Of course they will make it good.

Of course—"*bien entendu*"—"*por supuesto*"—

A hiss ran between I and the old photo phantoms—grind them up, spit them out and you'll feel better. They aren't *here*—way back in Paris, the café at the wrong corner. They grind—

"The mills of God grind slowly
but they grind exceeding small."

Right down to the atom and beyond.

Yes, let us accentuate the positive, and stop beefing about negative charge.

It's all part of some great big beautiful plan. You'll *love* it when you see it. It's the only way to live. A few chickens, a veg[etable] garden. All you need. Let's get down to basics, and beyond.

How dare Colt give me a defective snake?

So the flying serpent?

Rather awkward I think, but with some basic attractions.

Not too difficult. I mean the [pterodactyl] were what comes down—or up—to flying lizards, and it took about thirty feet of wingspan to get a 35-pound body, brain, mouth and teeth off the ground. Did the beast have talons like a hawk? Now just how long does it take before the feel of flight is born in the Dreaming Lizard?

It was a great concept, launched off cliffs to perilous missions.

"I can only exist in danger."

Without danger, I sag and wither.

What am I here for?

Writing—nothing.

So look out at the green trees and the blue sky.

[Why] were there so many arrowheads in Missouri farm fields? Did they miss that often?

July 9, 1997. Wednesday

Fletch died today.

The emptiness he leaves—the places where he used to be.

My Fletch, my Fletch.

The empty places where he used to be.

My Fletch, my Fletch!

This grief can kill.

My Fletch, My Fletch—

Can kill part of one.

T.P and Jim here. James later.

July 10, 1997. Thursday

Withal, Charles Henri Ford is possessed by an enigmatic, eerie charm, as a member of some spectral elite. He had the "mark" about him. The special thing. There is talk of the Devil's bargain. He is an individual.

July 11, 1997. Friday

"Time is a dimension," Wheeler says. (The Recognition Physics artist.)

So what the fuck is that supposed to mean?

"Told by an idiot, signifying nothing."

The Immortal Bard.

Miss Fletch so many times a day. Into kitchen this A.M., laid out three plates for cat food, and then it hits me. Only two now. "Must close door to front room, or Fletch will streak in and get under the bed." Don't bother shutting the door.

Literally miss. He isn't where he used to be, and never will be there again.

No trauma. His heart just gave out.

Wednesday A.M. he was lying on front porch. I put the food pan in front of him. He got up slow, started to eat.

Around 4:15 went out with T.P. to feed the fish. Fletch was lying just under the rear bumper of the old abandoned Datsun.

I guess I knew right away before T.P. told me:

"He's dead."

Move the chair closer to the bed, so he can jump easier onto the bed where he usually used to sleep.

It hurts every time. A physical pain, like phantom limb pain.

Bob McColl took the defective Colt Python away to be fixed or replaced. After all, it set me back eight hundred cool ones, and suppose I was depending on it for my very life and that python let me all the way down and some mutt beats my brains out with a pipe wrench? Now how would the Colt people feel about a thing like that?

I say it marks 'em lousy, and they better cover their ass and their assets STAT, and fast.

Luckily, I had a backup—Taurus snubby, .38 special.

July 13, 1997. Sunday

Well, book by a "former U.S. Marshall." *The Manhunter*. Pocket Star Books.

Need I say more. What a conflicted character this prick is, smokes pot, got a *dark side* to himself.

"Is that cop-killing puke going to get to Center alive?"

"I gave 'em my loyal services, now they want my *very soul!*"

"Sure, he tried to make a break for it, grabs my gun and I—uh—I—God, I had to do it! He'd gone berserk!"

(The Cop cracks up. Is led away sobbing.)

"Decent young cop. People just don't understand about cops. We're not all shits."

"They are animals!"—as the Mexican citizen classifies cops.

July 14, 1997. Monday

Appointment with John Barr M.D. aborted owing to lack of transport.

Took a bath this morning. The stanchions are essential.

How clean I feel. Mr. Clean.

Writer completes an age.

Arthritis slowly twisting and knobbing my fingers and elbows and shoulders, inexorable as limestone's slow deposit.

But I take heart: Cobra venom, Cobraxine, has—in certain cases—produced some remission, but the disturbing factor is that

Cobraxine may be addicting, relief consisting of satisfying an induced addiction.

A pre-induced addiction to Cobraxine. In this connection, an old snake feeler in Florida has taken an injection of Cobra venom—every day for sixty years. Unquestionably he is an addict.

Cobraxine was briefly used as a painkiller. Gold salts were also tried. Results were inconclusive, as results often are.

Reading about U.S. Marshall looking for Mengele. It seems he really died as described, in Brazil. He was swimming when a stroke hit the evil old bastard, who inhaled water and died. Attempts at reanimation were unsuccessful—and on the whole, ill-advised!

So here is the Cobra man—

He's got this T-shirt, lights up and swells the Cobra on his chest when he is holding, droops—pale green, shivering—in the Yen need. The vile hunger can eat a hole in the gut, and you better keep the worms down there, or it will ooze up inside and suddenly it grabs your mouth, feel it down in your teeth like a drill and—

Well, that's more or less it.

Unless you—or you or *tu* or *vous*—have anything to add or subtract, multiply or divide?

How I hated the math, the add + X. It was for me pure displeasure, which is not the way education should be. A round of displeasure culminating in involuntary football, under the idiot Coach Leland. Football was a cause, a religion to the Coach. Wonder what happened to the old Coach. Nothing of any meaning.

Kerouac—always referred to Tim Leary as "the Coach."

Shall I get a Devon Rex kitten. Difficult to let Ginger and Mutie in and out, and keep the kitten in.

Tim Leary as the Coach.

We are still in July 14, 1997

French Independence Day when they stormed the Bastille and sliced the Queen's head off. Stupid whore didn't know when it was time to leave and leave fast. She didn't leave fast enough.

"If they can't eat bread? Well, let them eat cake."

"Bad P.R., Lady, real bad."

"But I never . . ."

"Maybe not, but people *say* you said it. Comes to the same thing—maybe in the short run."

July 15, 1997. Tuesday

Late for—the *Marsellaise:*

[Les jours] de gloire sont—
Contre nous, les arcs levant—
Why not.
Sons of fear and sorrow.
Will you cheer tomorrow?
For the Whatever rhymes?
So? A war universe.
"It is all over."

Last words of Sri Aurobindo. He was in a trance for *twenty years?* (Maybe only ten, or even five.)

Then the Pondicherry Mother took over. She is (or was) French. The Pondicherry Mother. The Pond de Cheri Mother.

Mother, Mother, Mom.

Any case.

What remains after what is not here doesn't remain and why should it not remain.

"It was a big error," he said later, when it didn't matter any[thing] special now.

The pressure was now normal, and why yes—

"You can keep quite comfortable on Codeine."

"Do you know that men have been known to drop down dead for the timely want of opium / Prinavil?"

He gasps, doubled over in the hideous need of gastro-pancreatic spasms that can only be relieved by the sting of a rare scorpion, electric blue in color, emitting a stench of rotten ozone at the moment of the sting. Then retrenches into a neutral gray-brown, like some old piece of bark.

Anyone uses the term "bleeding heart" needs a bullet in his'n.

I am a bleeding heart. I bleed for lost kittens in hopeless alleys, the neglected, rejected of the disintegrating societal house of cards.

Be there a man
with soul so dead
never has throwed
himself on a bed
in aching spasms of
"If only—"
"Why didn't I—"
"Why did I—"
Grief like that hurts.

Hertz? 7 Hertz is said to be a very discombobulating—all right then, "upsetting" range—spectrum—heavy—

You know that yourself. Can burn out centers of fear & hate.

July 18, 1997. Friday

State of Hate of the Union.

So many [divisions] of America are sunked in the vilest spiritual ignorance, stupidity and basic [ill intentions] toward anything, any potential Homo Sap may harbor.

Yet here I sit and write this in comparative (to other countries) safety. I may add, precarious safety.

The powder trail is there. All it needs is one spark.

Yesterday [*Weekly World*] *News,* front-page story:

Timothy McVeigh reveals himself as a sniveling coward, cowering, weeping and screaming in his cell: "I don't wanta die!"

Hum. Not in any other papers. If they have faked it (most if not all of their news is faked), then they have perped a viler attack than his, to take from him any dignity and acceptance and eye-to-eye contact.

Now what Tim did was stupid, of course: sensibly he should have sought out the *individuals* responsible for Waco, and whacked them.

And look around for Ruby Ridgers when he was through.

Nobody cuddles up to baby killers, Tim. Bad P.R.

"Well, most of them was Jews."

"You think all federal agents are Jews?"

"Don't you *know?*"

Innocent bystanders, were they? Well, what are they doing there in the second place.

"After the fact?"

"She was full of reptiles."

J. Conrad, *Lord Jim.*

"[Four] bottles of that kind of brandy a day . . . should be dead, after such a festive experiment—tough old buzzard."

"You can keep quite comfortable on Codeine."

Old big-time pusher in Lexington. Seventy years old and you could see the prison years, other scenes and places. He was big-time in his day, I gather. Bob Ealeson? He came in with fat Saul, the *Schmecker* (that's a Yiddish word meaning drug-addicted).

"Don't have nothing to do with Saul, he's a *schmecker*."

(Purse mouth in distaste and disapproval.)

"A *schmecker!*"

It echoes through Jew bakeries, and restaurants and old-clothes bales, bursting open with musty bargains, smart moldy Italian jackets for the youth of the Azores and Madeira and—

—forget it.

"You can keep quite comfortable on Methadone."

It's a question of proportion in what you do, and even more in what you don't do.

Now here is a useful spirit exercise: Is there anything you would not do for *any* amount of money?

"Oh sure lotsa things. What good is big $$$ to me now? No time."

"Well now, we can fix that, Time Beast. How does Immortality hit you?"

"Don't take me for dumber than I look because I am (not in the short run)."

My hands and fingers, you see, have gone rebel on me.

Won't do what I tell them to do.

Whip them back in line, back into a fine ignorant line.

Well it's not much time—right—left.

July 19, 1997. Saturday

This arthritis is no joke.

Flash back. Hopeless alcoholic brother of Miggie, Mort's—my brother's—spouse, bored him twin girls. All right. Waye, the drunk, suddenly strode across the room and pulled down tufts of his ratty brown-gray hair.

"This drinking is no joke!"

Nobody was laughing.

Pick up book I am reading, called *Manhunter*, about U.S. Marshalls, and this phrase leaped out at me: "The plot sickens."

Takes me to Petronius and Trimalchio's feast:

"Ibat res ad summum nauseam."

"The thing was becoming perfectly sickening."

"Trimalchio now deep in the most vile drunkenness."

Miggie says: "Uh huh."

Waye goes back and sits down.

He died I guess.

They all died. Mort and Miggie.

Let's not get morbid.

Remember that atrocious Spanish-American War, I mean the songs of that war:

"Came a cry from every Captain:
'Look boys, our flag is down
Who'll volunteer to
save it from distress?'
'I will,' a young boy shouted
'I'll bring it back or die.'
Saved the flag but gave his young life
all for his country's sake—
'Just break the news to mother
and say there'll be no other

But tell her not to wait for me,
'cause I'm not coming home.'"

What loathsome treacle from the cauldrons of dull—
Appalling to think anyone could have delivered such [muck]—
"Cold and wet but it burns, see, such a caustic exudant to seek out and dissolve any remnant of real thought and feeling and sensory impressions."
"It's all over."
"*Quién es?*"
"He'll quail before a good woman's gauze—gaze—"

Lost it there. Well, better check your assets.
Mother, Dad, Mort, Billy—I failed them all—
And Ruski the actor.
Can any actor fill the *living role?* Many are called, few squeeze through.
So where and when and why is obvious. What every school boy knows:
"Those to whom evil is done, do evil in return." Wystan Auden.

How easy the new S&W .22 8-shot slides out one to the head. Can mean end of argument.

July 20, 1997. Sunday

They say a writer should have something he does with his hands (besides typing, that is). Pulling cat hairs from the Hudson Bay blanket seems to be my hand thing. That and shooting. I groom her, but the hairs are seemingly inexhaustible. What's a man to do. Ain't got no chance, one man alone.

Stumbles on a vile deed: report in the *Weekly [World] News*. McVeigh has turned into a sniveling coward, sobbing: "I don't want to die."

Has he? No responsible newspaper has reported what is certainly a newsworthy event. Only the *Weekly News* has culled this scoop from its mysterious "sources." I nominate the *Weekly News* for the Vilest Act of the Century. If this story is fabricated, the *News* has perpetrated—has extended the very frontiers of vileness.

I remember the Machos. Died smoking. Mexican *banditos* stand against a pitted adobe wall, sneering at the firing squad.

So some reporter *who wasn't even there* reports:

"The bandits died begging for their lives. Most of them lost control of their bowels and bladders."

I was there. I will hunt that rat reporter down. I will force him to beg for his life *in front of witnesses,* promising to spare his life if he begs for it like Fido on his knees, with little yips while the cameras roll.

Lights, action, (pistol shots), camera.

To me the most unforgivable sin is the Lie, because like counterfeit currency, it devalues truth.

He has endured tortures that would have reduced most men to sniveling wrecks, an agent of a service so secret it can never be admitted to exist. Now he is, by computer magic, suddenly "a dirty child-molesting dope fiend," spit on and pelted with rocks from snarling children.

He's had all he can take.

"Fill my truck with ammonium nitrate. I'm going to fertilize till the land looks level."

Few survive the Big Switch.
So then?
Straight-aheadedness.

July 21, 1997. Monday

It was a Monday, 1882.

"That picture's awful dusty."

Jesse James took off his gun belt to dust off *The Death of Stonewall Jackson*. Bob Ford shot and killed him.

The Old West. What a bore. Still, the gun fight was a spiritual exercise, like sword fighting and fencing [and] bull fighting. The gun fighter puts his life on the line. After you win, it's a sweet clean feeling like being borned, they tell me—never been there myself.

Now is nothing left.

So maybe one will finally stop looking at the cloth, and see who—what—is behind the cloth.

That will be the day.

July 23, 1997. Wednesday

So what will happen so special?

St. Christopher is the patron saint of travelers, drifters, adventurers, explorers, gentlemen of the road and beyond.

Guides to fictitious places desperately fill in the details:

"Need some *young boys* in here STAT, and mature whores in hula skirts and miles of white sand beaches and palms trees."

"No fucking land crabs or centipedes or scorpions. Nice clean set."

Where's the danger then? Where's the *friction?* Where is the *energy?*

Well, some evil influence is trying to fuck up the clean set. Could be old Ctulhu, the dirty Old Ones. So some hero must oppose the ultimate vileness that dare not squeak its name, like a rat.

So we drag it out a few more reels, but it's a *sick picture*.

The stage is getting darker.

Just can't do it no more, it's all the sane—

John D.C.—"All the same—sane." Well, John D.C. in his letters keeps saying: "It's all the sane." So what that mean in the code?

Nothing.

So what.

"To die, perhaps to dream—aye, there's the rub."

"To be or not to be

there is the question."

Yes, the Bard exhausted so many potentials. So many book titles he has delivered: *The Sound and the Fury. All Our Yesterdays. Told by an Idiot.*

It would be a very small man to attack the Immortal Bard. A thousand, a million, a billion pens will sputter in his defense, tap out on the old rented typewriter.

Yes, I remember when the agent for the typewriter rental agency came to reclaim my typewriter. This was in Mexico City. He had no way to know who I was, but wasn't at that time, and he said:

"When you pay good, okay. When you pay *malo*, is no good."

He repossessed the typewriter and departed forever from my sight. He was middle-aged, gray hair, no hostility in him.

Old dust of dead people and places.

Enter transformed
Writer.

At his beck and call great shambling beasts, with the claws of bears, and the teeth of Mandrills.

What?

Remember pilot was driven onto his wing by a Mandrill, and both went to [their] glory.

Oh well. Why think about that? A bad apple.

It happens. A bad apple.

Could there be good apples if there were never any *bad* apples.

The Ugly American fading out in Ewyork, Ome, Aris—

Even uglier were summoned:

"Dissidence must be put down with an iron fist."

July 26, 1997. Saturday

Dick says Angelo will turn in time. "Everyone does," he says.

"Drug addicts are the best people I know."

—Book reading now: *Junk,* by Linda Yablonsky, N.Y.C.

Comparatively harmless, and they have absorbed—literally—some basic [metabolic] lessons. They know more about life than the squares, like my unfortunate brother.

Spent a year in Paris. He said about bidets (the typical American comment): "I don't like the idea."

July 27, 1997. Sunday

The cuteness disease.

Ambassador chewing on a hay stalk. FBI agent patting gun.

"It's a terrible thing when a man—"

—has hairs growing on the backs of his fingers, black hairs crisscross a vulgar great diamond ring . . . the guard at Lecumberri Federal Prison in Mexico D.F.—

"It's a bad thing when a man comes to the prison because of a woman."

And he gives me a *real human look*. It's a look you don't get from American guards, with beer potbellies and cold gray eyes, pale, cold and dirty—like ice sludge.

Recollect from Lexington, the three old-timers came in together. Saul, a Jew; Bob, seventy years old, trim, dignified, did a nickel in Leavenworth for big-time junk sales; and Chuck, small, thin.

"It's the junky gets it in the belly for something he can't help. A junky is *born* a junky. And nobody ever gets anybody on junk except the junky himself."

Saul: "They all say 'Don't have anything to do with Saul. He's a *schmecker*.'"

Yiddish word for junky, derived from or giving rise to "Smack."

Told about encounter with Wilson, a faceless bureaucrat. I can't *see* his face. Just gray coat, and something cold and dead in there. He didn't question me, Faulkner did, William's brother turned revenooer, turned Fed.

Once the agents got talking among themselves the way agents will, and Wilson comes in—he was always coming in or going out and leaving a sucking emptiness behind or bringing it in— now he brought it in.

He points to me, not looking at me—he never looked at me— and said:

"Is he a *violator!*"

And all the agents shut up. A violator shouldn't hear agent shop talk.

But back to Saul and his encounter with Wilson:

"He is asking me for names, addresses, walking down a hall and finally I say: *'Awww,'*"—(and he could *Awww* ugly)—"'why don't you ask your mother?' And I was sorry after I said it. He kicked me in the ribs, fractures, bound up in tape for a month."

Old gray Bob.

Some New York hustler is talking about a drunk at a subway platform—

Bob: "Why didn't you slam him back against the bench and take it off him?"

The effect was grotesque and dislocating, like it was grated out by a friend of my father's who was a bank president. Bob had a natural dignity about him.

And he said: "You can keep quite comfortable on Codeine."

Memories of Lexington. I hear now the inmates get *nothing*. When I went in, I got a quarter [g] of morphine, and five milligrams of Methadone. I was stoned. [Had] been in kick city for four lousy days. And all the St. Louis croakers too chicken to give me even a lousy quarter g. That was when things were tough—real tough.

So when I got to Lex—my mother screaming behind me she had some idea I should go to a private nuthouse—and I said:

"All I need is [a] withdrawal cure. Period."

And she was very annoyed by me and Joan taking the bull by the horns and opting for Lexington.

Mother said about Joan: "She was just like a *tigress*." Said no to any enforced confinement.

She was right there, and other where's and there's.

What can I say—

Why who where when can I say—

Tears are worthless unless genuine, tears from the soul and the guts, tears that ache and wrench and hurt and tear.

Tears for what was—

The way Fletch used to run into the front room and get under the bed and now—well, I don't have to keep the door closed now.

My Fletch, my Fletch—

It hurts, these pieces of myself and Fletch, like phantom limbs.

Putting out the feed bowls, only need two now.
Oh my Fletch—
My Spooner, Ruski, Calico.

July 28, 1997. Monday

The doctor needed more blood from me for his *tests*.

I gave it this morning.

If one is immortal, imagine the pain of loss, again and again, as others die.

So one has comparative immortality *vis-a-vis* his cats. Note that the most painful twinges are delivered by annoying bits— the way Fletch streaked into the front room and got under the bed, he'll never do that again. The way Calico used to scream in the afternoon. Those cries will never be heard again. They will never annoy you again.

Imagine—that is, see, look at—centuries of that.

For what? Or who? And *surtout pourquoi?*

Why? Yes, no, why not?

Last words of Tim Leary:

"Why not?"

July 29, 1997. Tuesday

Good shooting.

July 30, 1997. Wednesday

Reading *Titanic* by Charles Pellegrino. Page 18.

What is an experience if it is not shared? Did it even happen? It takes another person to form an—(postcard with cute kittens falls into waste basket. Must have slid down slow?)—experience. As a screen. That is why God had to create.

Otherwise?

A centipede can be seen as a test upon which Love, like St. Francis used to make, would shatter.

There must be a "place of failure." What life can survive an atomic blast?

(Psychoanalysis is attempt to defuse an experience by sharing. Hmmm. That is, by making the experience real enough to kill it. Hardly ever works.)

Atom bomb is the ultimate soul killer, that vaporizes all debts as it vaporized the steel tower at Alamogordo, New Mexico.

(Fat soul.)

"Our vegetable love will grow, vaster than empires and more slow."

No idea where or why that quote came from. Know the whole poem, of course, brain littered up with old bits and pieces.

"Pieces of eight!" screamed the parrot.

Wouldn't you, if you were a parrot had learned how?

Felicity [Mason], describing me to someone holding tickets I needed:

"When you see someone who looks like the saddest man in the world, that's him."

How can a man who *sees* and *feels* be other than sad.

To see Ginger always older and weaker.

The price of immortality, of course.

Well, you should have thought of these things.

I did. Thinking is not enough.

Nothing is. There is no final enough of wisdom, experience—any fucking thing. No Holy Grail, No Final Satori, no final solution. Just conflict.

Only thing can resolve conflict is love, like I felt for Fletch and Ruski, Spooner and Calico. Pure love.

What I feel for my cats present and past.

Love? What is It?

Most natural painkiller what there is.

LOVE.

NOTES for *Last Words*
Aug. 31, 1999

November 14, 1996

Tom Peschio was a close friend and one of Burroughs's Lawrence companions. It was he who came upon Burroughs in his home during his fatal heart attack nine months later, on August 1, 1997.

November 15, 1996

heart doc: Burroughs had an appointment with one of his cardiologists this afternoon.

Qui vivre verra: "Who lives will see," a favorite of Burroughs's maxims.

November 18, 1996

Herbert Huncke, 81: Huncke died the previous summer, on August 8, 1996.

Dr. Dent: James Yerbury Dent administered an apomorphine cure to Burroughs in London in 1956.

November 19, 1996

Harris Construction: Burroughs's home phone number was different by one digit from that of a local construction company.

Lexington Narc hospital: Burroughs stayed at the Federal narcotics hospital in Lexington, Kentucky, in 1946 to attempt a cure for his heroin addiction.

November 20, 1996

Victor Bockris, a writer who met Burroughs in New York in 1974, wrote a biographical portrait of him in the 1980s (*With William Burroughs: A Report from the Bunker*), and remained friends to the end.

José Férez is an art dealer and poet who often worked in Lawrence and was one of Burroughs's frequent companions.

My creeping opponents: Burroughs delivered these remarks several days later, at the "Nova Convention Revisited" event at the University of Kansas in Lawrence on November 26, 1996. The event was part of the "Ports of Entry" exhibition at the University's Helen Foresman Spencer Museum of Art that same month.

November 29, 1996

Herr Professor Federn: Psychoanalyst Paul Federn was a pupil of Freud's; he treated Burroughs in New York in 1941.

Chestnut Lodge, in Maryland, is a psychiatric institution where Burroughs was evaluated for discharge from the U.S. Army in 1942.

November 30, 1996

Dr. *Schlumberger* was Burroughs's psychoanalyst for a short time in Paris in 1958.

Lottery Building: Burroughs and his lover Ian Sommerville lived in a small penthouse at the Lotería building in Tangier in 1964.

December 2, 1996

Brion Gysin (1916–1986), painter and writer, was Burroughs's closest friend and collaborator, in Tangier, Paris, and New York.

English writer *Denton Welch* (1915–1948) was acknowledged by Burroughs as an important literary influence.

December 9, 1996

James McCrary was a friend and companion to Burroughs from 1991, and is the office manager of William Burroughs Communications in Lawrence.

December 13, 1996

James Grauerholz was Burroughs's companion from 1974 until Burroughs's death and is the executor of his estate.

Michael ("*Mikey*") *Portman* (1945?–1983) was an admirer of Burroughs in London who became friends with him in 1960.

December 14, 1996

Burroughs Family story: Burroughs's father, Mortimer Perry Burroughs, was a teenager when WSB I died, in 1898, and he retained all or most of his inherited Burroughs Company stock;

reportedly Mortimer sold his last part of it just before the 1929 stock market crash.

Yagé mucho da: "*yagé* give much," incanted by the brujo as he prepares the *yagé*.

December 20, 1996

Ed Anger: Burroughs often read the tabloid *Weekly World News* for amusement; "Ed Anger" is a *News* columnist specializing in the "mad-as-hell/sound-off" style.

December 21, 1996

T.P. = Tom Peschio

December 22, 1996

David and Sue: David Ohle and Susan Brosseau were friends of Burroughs in Lawrence; beginning in the early 1990s, David and Wayne Propst made a weekly dinner visit on Thursdays.

December 28, 1996

Dr. Senseny and his family were neighbors of Burroughs's family in the Central West End of St. Louis in the 1920s.

Valley Ranch: although Burroughs attended a preparatory school in Los Alamos, New Mexico, called Los Alamos Ranch School, from September 1929 to April 1931, this reference appears to be to a dude ranch in New Mexico where he went with his mother as a young child.

December 29, 1996

Cabell Lee Hardy was Burroughs's companion in Boulder, Colorado, in the late 1970s, and they remained friends thereafter.

The so-called *Beat Hotel* was a rooming hotel at 9, rue Git-le-Coeur in Paris, where Burroughs and Gysin and many other writers and painters lived in the late 1950s and early '60s.

Oppenheimer: The correct J. Robert Oppenheimer quote, from the *Bhagavad Gita,* is: "I am become Death, destroyer of worlds."

January 10, 1997

Roger Holden was a friend of Burroughs in the Lawrence years.

January 14, 1997

Ted: Ted Morgan was Burroughs's first biographer (*Literary Outlaw,* Henry Holt and Co., 1988).

January 17, 1997

John Grigsby Geiger is a Canadian writer who has been working for some years on a biography of Brion Gysin.

"Towers, Open Fire": is a quote from a short film (1963) of the same name by Burroughs and Antony Balch, who was a close friend and collaborator with Burroughs in the 1960s and '70s, mostly in London.

John Hopkins is a British writer who was a friend of Burroughs in Tangier in the 1960s.

Robert Filliou (1926–1987) was an artist; in the 1960s he was a member of the Fluxus Group and the Domaine Poetique (Poesie Sonore) in Paris.

Ian Sommerville (1941–1976) was a mathematician and engineer who was Burroughs's companion from 1959 to 1965, in Paris, Tangier, and London.

January 24, 1997

Shein & O'Grady: Burroughs was arrested in April 1946 in New York for forging a narcotics prescription.

January 29, 1997

I drove Joan to the hospital: Joan Vollmer (1924–1951), Burroughs's common-law wife from 1947 until her accidental death (Burroughs shot her) four years later, gave birth to their son, William S. ("Billy") Burroughs, Jr., on July 21, 1947 at a hospital in Conroe, Texas. Billy was raised by Burroughs's parents, Mortimer and Laura Lee Burroughs, first in St. Louis, then in Palm Beach, Florida. Burroughs visited his son every year or two, and lived near him in Boulder, Colorado, in the late 1970s following Billy's liver transplant in 1976. Mortimer and Laura Burroughs died in 1965 and 1970, respectively. Billy died in 1981.

Maître Bumsell was a French lawyer hired by Burroughs to deal with a narcotics investigation targeting him in Paris in 1959. (Maître—"master"—is an appellation.)

Franklin Street: Burroughs's second address in New York after his return from Europe was 77 Franklin Street, third floor, where he lived from June 1974–May 1976.

pain in gut: For the last five or six years of his life Burroughs suffered intermittent painful stomach reflux from a hiatal hernia.

January 30, 1997

Nichols': Burroughs's made a bi-weekly trip to the methadone clinic in Kansas City on Thursday mornings. Afterward he would almost always eat breakfast at Nichols' Lunch on Southwest Trafficway.

January 31, 1997

Robert Sudlow is an acclaimed Kansas landscape painter with whom Burroughs was friendly.

Anne Oliver and Eugene Angert were childhood classmates of Burroughs at the John Burroughs School in St. Louis in the late 1920s. *David Kammerer* was also from St. Louis; he was three years older than Burroughs.

February 3, 1997

Horn . . . The Club of Rome: Burroughs is referring to a speaker at the annual conference of the Ecotechnics Institute in Aix-en-Provence, France, at which he also spoke, in the early 1980s.

February 6, 1997

Sue Lowe was a friend of Burroughs from the late 1970s. Her twin brother Steven Lowe was also a close friend and lived in Lawrence during 1991–93.

February 7, 1997

"travel around and be cruel": Burroughs is quoting Jerome ("Jerry") Wallace, whom he met as a young man in Paris in the late 1950s.

February 9, 1997
Bradford Morrow, novelist and editor of the literary magazine *Conjunctions*, had invited Burroughs to submit a short piece for a collection he was compiling.

February 25, 1997
Pharr, Texas: Burroughs and his friend since childhood, Kells Elvins, bought and farmed land together near Pharr in 1946–47.

March 1, 1997
210 Centre St.: Burroughs lived in New York City for a year in 1964–65, most of that time at this address in a sublet loft.

Harvard: Burroughs attended Harvard University from 1932–36.

March 3, 1997
"We'll meet again" etc.: Burroughs refers here to the ending of Stanley Kubrick's 1964 film, *Dr. Strangelove or: How I Learned to Stop Worrying and Love the Bomb*, with Vera Lynn singing "We'll Meet Again" over a montage of aerial footage of hydrogen-bomb bursts. The song was popular during WW II.

Carl Laszlo is an art dealer based in Basel whom Burroughs met in New York and visited at his home in Switzerland in the 1980s.

March 10, 1997
Venice . . . Alan and I: Burroughs traveled from New York to meet writer Alan Ansen in Rome in early 1954, on his way to Tangier.

March 11, 1997

Commander of Arts and Letters: Burroughs was awarded the honor of a Commandeur de l'Ordre des Arts et des Lettres of France in 1984 by minister of culture Jacques Lang, at Bourges.

March 22, 1997

Poet *Allen Ginsberg* (1926–1997) was a lifelong friend of Burroughs, beginning in the mid-1940s. Together with Jack Kerouac, they are considered the founders of the Beat generation.

there I am in East St. Louis: During 1932–43, on trips home from Harvard and after his graduation in 1936, Burroughs would explore the red-light "Valley district" of East St. Louis, sometimes with his friend David Kammerer or the much younger Lucien Carr, on whom Kammerer had a fatal fixation.

I was teaching: In the spring of 1974 Burroughs returned to New York from London to teach a seminar class on creative writing at the City College of New York; he ended up staying in the city until 1982.

March 24, 1997

The Wishing Machine is a psycho-electronic device that can hold a small photo or object and be used to focus the wisher's intention.

bottle of Absolut: In March 1997 the Absolut Vodka company was talking with Burroughs's agents about the possibility of his doing an ad for them, featuring his artwork—i.e., "Absolut Burroughs"—as several of his artist friends, including Keith Haring, had already done. The project did not work out.

March 28, 1997

John T. Lee was a close friend of James Grauerholz in Lawrence; he was also acquainted with Burroughs, who stayed in Lee's downtown apartment during his first visit to Lawrence, a four-day residency with the University of Kansas in 1976. Lee died at age 51 on March 27, 1997.

April 1, 1997

the Heidsiecks: performance poet Bernard Heidsieck (related to the Heidsieck champagne company) and his wife Françoise, a photographer, both of them friends of Burroughs' since the 1960s, were visiting from Paris that week.

April 2, 1997

Piper Do: The mass suicide of the "Heaven's Gate" cult in California occurred at this time.

April 3, 1997

Bill Gilmore: William S. Gilmore was a friend of Burroughs and a fellow Harvard alum; they were associated in New York in 1939–40.

April 9, 1997

Fred Baxter: may refer to Burroughs's housemaster at Harvard.

April 10, 1997

Kansas City with Wayne: Wayne Propst, Burroughs's friend in Lawrence and a Thursday-night regular, volunteered to take Grauerholz's place on the clinic trip this day.

April 11, 1997

Vail Ennis, Sheriff: Burroughs and Joan Vollmer were arrested in Beeville, Texas, in 1947, having sex in their car by the side of the road on their way from Pharr to New Waverly, Texas, where they had a farm.

M.S.: morphine sulfate.

Little Jack Melody was a small-time thief who was associated with Burroughs and Ginsberg in New York in the late 1940s; it was with Melody that Ginsberg had participated in the car chase in 1949 that resulted in his arrest and eventual commitment to the Columbia Presbyterian Psychiatric Institute in New York.

April 12, 1997

Pat Connor was among the circle of Lawrence friends who visited Burroughs and prepared his evening meal on a regular basis.

April 13, 1997

copains: Grauerholz and poet John Giorno, who was a close friend of Burroughs in New York since the mid-1960s until the end of Burroughs's life, were returning to Lawrence by car from Springfield, Missouri, where Giorno had given a reading that weekend. When they arrived in the late afternoon, Burroughs reported he had apparently suffered a mild heart attack. His cardiologist was immediately contacted and, as he was stable at that point, an appointment was made for the next day. Burroughs had written some lines on the bottom of this journal page that he evidently intended as possibly his "last words," but he later tore out the lower half of the page.

April 19, 1997

to record Jim Morrison: producer Ralph Sall recorded Burroughs reading a Morrison poem for a Doors tribute album project.

April 20, 1997

Dr. Richard Orchard is a respected Lawrence ophthalmologist. He made annual examinations of Burroughs's eyesight, and performed a successful cataract-removal procedure on him on Monday, April 21, 1997. This greatly improved Burroughs's vision and his aim with a pistol, increasing his enjoyment of the frequent shooting outings.

April 22, 1997

Linda was one of Burroughs's favorite nurses at the methadone clinic in Kansas City.

April 26, 1997

my bond salesman cousin, Robert Hoxie: Robert L. Hoxie (1903–1940). See also entry for May 8, 1997.

April 28, 1997

Professor *George Wedge* of the University of Kansas English Department became friends with Burroughs in the early 1980s when he invited him to address his class on the literature of addiction. In the fall of 1987, Wedge co-produced the "River City Reunion," with Bill Rich and James Grauerholz. For many years Wedge edited the student literary magazine, *Cottonwood Review.*

Vale: editor and cultural historian V. Vale of San Francisco was a longtime friend of Burroughs.

"*a* kindly *ruin*": Burroughs was often visited at his Kansas home by pilgrims, some by arrangement, some out of the blue. One of these young visitors wrote up the encounter for a little magazine and used this phrase to describe Burroughs.

Vancouver, age 79: Burroughs's last trip to Vancouver, B.C., was in summer 1988, when he was 74.

April 30, 1997

Doctor Kurt Eissler, M.D.: Burroughs consulted psychiatrist Kurt Eissler (1908–1999) for a short time in Chicago in 1942–43.

May 2, 1997

"*bank for a closing*": Burroughs was purchasing some vacant acreage near Lone Star Lake, south of Lawrence, from his friend Steven Lowe.

Pine Valley, Texas: In 1947–48 Burroughs and Vollmer lived on a farm near New Waverly, Texas, in the neighborhood of Cold Springs and Pine Valley.

ortalon: a fulsome French delicacy, tiny birds prepared by rotting and eaten with a large napkin over the gourmet's head.

May 3, 1997

The caviar arrived: Burroughs enjoyed salty snacks with his afternoon cocktail of vodka and Coke, and his favorite was caviar or, more often, red salmon eggs. These delicacies were delivered by courier, packed in dry ice.

James Le Baron Boyle: James Louis Le Blanc Boyle II was a classmate of Burroughs at Harvard.

May 4, 1997

A. J. Connell was the founder and director of the Los Alamos Ranch School in the 1920s and 1930s.

May 8, 1997

Mr. Faulkner: Burroughs was arrested in New Orleans in 1949 and charged with drugs and weapons possession. He was jailed and later hospitalized.

Waid's: When Burroughs did not have his after-clinic breakfast at Nichols' Lunch, he went to this nearby diner.

May 9, 1997

Paul Swann: This athlete and figure model billed himself as "The Most Beautiful Man in the World," but Swann was well past his prime when Burroughs and Kells Elvins attended a presentation of Swann's physique at a private salon in New York in the late 1930s. Burroughs's ill-suppressed giggling caused the two of them to be ejected from the viewing.

Señor Kaposi: This is the title of a short piece of fiction by Burroughs which was published in a catalog for Giorno Poetry Systems' line of spoken-word records.

May 10, 1997

Maurice Girodias (1919–1990) was the pioneering publisher of The Olympia Press in Paris in the 1950s and '60s; he published the first edition of Burroughs's breakthrough novel, *Naked Lunch,* in 1959.

May 11, 1997

Went out to Fred's and shot very well: Fred Aldrich was a close friend of Burroughs in Lawrence; his farm, a few miles northwest of town, was the scene of countless target-shooting excursions by Burroughs and other friends during the last decade of Burroughs's life.

May 12, 1997

Must see Charlie Kincaid: Charles Kincaid was Burroughs's personal dentist for many years; he is a sympathetic and modern individual, who appreciated Burroughs as a writer and as a friend.

May 15, 1997

Prince's Square: From 1960 to 1974 Burroughs lived for the most part in London. A hotel at 7, Prince's Square, Bayswater, was his address for two weeks in 1964. *Boots's* was the chemist where Burroughs and many other addicts would fill their legal heroin scripts; Burroughs was also prescribed a gram of hashish per week, which he obtained at this pharmacy.

May 17, 1997

the left-behind Sneer: This is a gay "zine," published in Kansas City since the late 1990s; the copy Burroughs was looking for included an interview profile of Grauerholz.

May 23, 1997

ME TOO Band: The Irish rock band U2 invited Burroughs to act in a music video of "Last Night on Earth," a song from their latest CD. The filming tied up traffic in downtown Kansas City for several hours. Burroughs portrayed a shopping-cart person in a smart black suit, with a huge klieg light in his cart. (Actually occurred on Thursday, May 22, 1997.)

May 29, 1997

Bob Marsden was a classmate of Burroughs at the Los Alamos Ranch School.

May 31, 1997

Doug and Stephanie: Douglas Grant and Stephanie Williams were friends of Burroughs whom he'd met through their work in a Magickal order known as "I.O.T.," into which Burroughs was initiated by them and Stephanie's husband Bob in the early 1990s.

June 2, 1997

cars . . . Learnard: Burroughs lived from 1983 until his death at 1927 Learnard Avenue in Lawrence.

June 6, 1997

Bill Willis was a wealthy and flamboyant interior decorator who hosted Burroughs in his lavish home in Marrakesh while Burroughs was writing *The Wild Boys* in the late 1960s.

June 7, 1997

David Budd (d. 1990) was a painter whom Burroughs had met in Paris in the 1960s. Budd spent his life around the "circus world" of Sarasota, Florida, and this friendship led Burroughs to write *The Last Words of Dutch Schultz*. The two men remained close friends until Budd's death.

June 15, 1997

"Gloomy Sunday" was recorded by Billie Holiday in 1941, but its message was so dark it was shunned by the music industry generally.

Skeptical Inquirer: This is a newsletter specializing in debunking reports of paranormal phenomena. A friend of Burroughs sent him a gift subscription, thinking he would enjoy it, not realizing how deeply Burroughs was committed to the idea of a "magical universe."

June 17, 1997

Primate Center: After developing a keen interest in lemurs in the mid-1980s, Burroughs visited the Duke University Primate Center in North Carolina with his friend William H. Rich in 1989. He included a fund-raising appeal for D.U.P.C. in his 1995 book *Ghost of Chance.*

fishing trip, Montana: Burroughs's father Mortimer took him and his older brother, Mortimer, Jr., on an excursion to Missoula when they were children.

June 20, 1997

The actor: This refers to actor Steve Buscemi, whose performance in the Coen brothers' film, "Fargo," Burroughs watched on video in preparation for a visit by Buscemi to Lawrence beginning the next day, for talks about a film version of *Junky* combined with *Queer*.

June 22, 1997
Ilse Herzfeld Klapper was a Jewish intellectual from Hamburg whom Burroughs met in Dubrovnik in 1936–37 and married at the U.S. Consulate in Athens on August 2, 1937.

June 24, 1997
Mary Cooke and her husband John were early adherents of L. Ron Hubbard and founded the Church of Scientology based on Hubbard's principles of "Dianetics." Burroughs (and Gysin) knew Mary Cooke in Tangier in the 1950s.

June 30, 1997
Charles Henri Ford was an avant-garde prodigy and for many years the protégé of émigré painter Pavel Chelitchew. With Parker Tyler, Ford wrote *The Young and Evil,* a novel about gay expatriate life in Paris in the 1920s. He founded the literary magazine *View* around that time, and stayed active in letters thereafter. A famous photograph of Burroughs was taken by Ford in Paris in the late 1950s.

Fred Sparks was a news photographer and bon vivant, of Ford's and Burroughs's mutual acquaintance.

July 4, 1997
Baron Franz von Blomberg: William P. Frere von Blomberg, a Harvard classmate of Burroughs.

a real friend? . . . your cat: Burroughs's longtime veterinarian, Dr. John Bradley, made a house call on this day to examine Fletch, who had persistent gastrointestinal distress and was obese. The cat appeared to be fairly well and his blood tests were normal on that day, so his sudden death five days later was unexpected. (After Burroughs died, his friend Tom Peschio devotedly cared for his two surviving cats in the home for a year and a half, until Ginger and Mutie died of natural causes.)

July 8, 1997

I am calling McColl: Robert McColl, a professor at the University of Kansas, was a gun enthusiast and friend of Burroughs and helped him buy and sell several handguns over the years.

July 11, 1997

The Recognition Physics artist: John Wheeler is a physicist who has written about his concept of "recognition physics," which postulates that for something to exist it must be perceived; Burroughs was taken with this idea.

July 14, 1997

John Barr, M.D., was Burroughs's personal internist in Lawrence for several years. The "lack of transport" occurred because Burroughs had not alerted any of his helpers to the impending appointment until a half hour beforehand.

stanchions are essential: Burroughs is referring to wall-mounted grab-bars around his bathtub, which were installed for him by Wayne Propst.

July 27, 1997

Lecumberri Federal Prison: Burroughs was incarcerated for eleven days in Lecumberri Prison in Mexico City after he accidentally shot Joan Vollmer, on September 6, 1951.

Old gray Bob: Bob Brandenburg was a tough small-time crook whom Burroughs had known and admired in New York in the mid-1940s.

July 29, 1997

Good shooting: Burroughs's last target-shooting trip to Fred Aldrich's farm was this day.